Embroidery Tips

Embroidery Tips

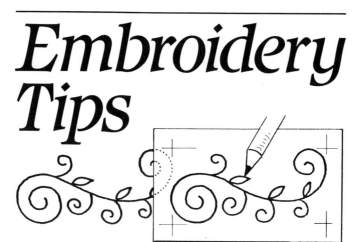

GRETE PETERSEN

VNR VAN NOSTRAND REINHOLD COMPANY

Broderitips copyright © 1982 by Grete Petersen and Høst & Søns Forlag
Translation copyright © 1984 by Van Nostrand Reinhold Company Inc.
Library of Congress Catalog Card Number 83-23354

ISBN 0-442-27463-7

Printed in the United States of America
Designed by Diane Saxe

Illustrations by the author

Translation by Carol L. Schroeder

Published by Van Nostrand Reinhold Company Inc.
135 West 50th Street
New York, New York 10020

Van Nostrand Reinhold Company Limited
Molly Millars Lane
Wokingham, Berkshire RG11 2PY, England

Van Nostrand Reinhold
480 La Trobe Street
Melbourne, Victoria 3000, Australia

Macmillan of Canada
Division of Gage Publishing Limited
164 Commander Boulevard
Agincourt, Ontario M1S 3C7, Canada

16 15 14 13 12 11 10 9 8 7 6 5 4 3 2 1

Library of Congress Cataloging in Publication Data

Petersen, Grete.
   Embroidery tips.

   Translation of: Broderitips.
   Includes index.
   1. Embroidery.   2. Needlework.   I. Title.
TT770.P47813   1984   746.44   83-23354
ISBN 0-442-27463-7

Contents

Introduction	vi
Practical Advice	1
Materials	2
The Care of Finished Embroidery	5
Pattern Design	6
Corners	12
Seams and Edge Treatments	14
Decorative Seams	18
Fringes and Pompons	20
Cross-Stitch	22
Alternatives to Cross-Stitch	24
Pillows	26
Bell Pulls	28
Wall Hangings	29
Handbags	30
Alphabets	35
Patterns	38
The Placement of Embroidery	41
Embroidery on Knitting	42
Inspirations from Old Embroidery	44
Free-style Embroidery	48
Embroidery Based on Children's Drawings	50
Patchwork	52
Embroidery in Relief	56
Pictures from Fabric Scraps	58
Quilting	60
Embroidery on Clothing	64
Beadwork	68
Dolls	70
Index	72

Introduction

Considering the amount of time it takes to complete a piece of handwork, it's obviously a good idea to spend a bit of it on correct preparation so that the end result will be as good as you had hoped.

This reference book should help you get things just right. It gives tips on materials and techniques and offers suggestions for easy sewing projects that can be fun to do right away. It discusses how embroidery can be used on fabrics and on pieces of clothing. It covers how to find patterns, combine them, and apply them. In addition, there are a few ideas for recycling various materials into new projects.

This book is for both the beginner and the more advanced craftsperson, but of course its size limits how much can be covered in each section. So if one of the types of embroidery described is of particular interest, consult more specialized reference books.

Practical Advice

Sit in a relaxed but upright position in a chair that is the correct height for you and has good back support. Light should fall on the work from the left (or from the right if you are left-handed). Poor posture or inadequate light will have a negative effect on your finished work.

While sewing, take care that you don't crush the fabric so much that it wrinkles. Hold the work in your left hand (or in your right hand if you are left-handed). Lay the fabric over your index and middle fingers, holding it with the other three fingers. When embroidering, stretch the fabric between the fingers so that it lies flat. This is particularly important if two identical pieces are to be sewn together. Hold the embroidery needle between your right-hand thumb and index finger. When using a thimble, place it on the middle finger. This finger can also be used to play out the thread (1-1). Don't hold onto the thread and pull on it—that takes more time. The thread should not be too long, with one exception: when sewing a piece in which there can't be any fastening off at an end.

Never begin with a knot. If you leave the end loose on the front of the fabric it can later be fastened down. Change threads as inconspicuously as possible. For example, when tacking down the end of a row of chain stitches, let one loop remain (1-2) and hold onto it while attaching the end of the old thread and the beginning of the new thread on the back of the fabric; then come up through this loop with the new thread (1-3).

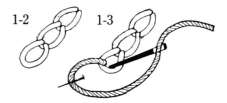

To make embroidery easier, first pull the floss through your fingers: this takes some of the twist out of it and makes it more cooperative. If the thread starts to twist up and develops a tendency toward knotting while you are embroidering, let the needle and thread hang loose from the fabric until it has untwisted itself again.

It can be well worth your while to work a test swatch of embroidery. With counted thread work it can be particularly helpful to sew a sample of ten stitches, for example, to find out

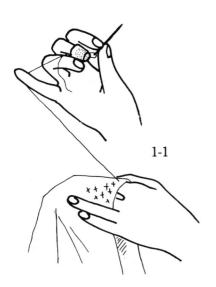

1-1

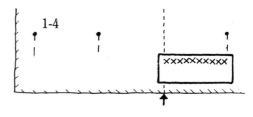

how large an area the embroidery will fill, how many threads of fabric should be covered by each stitch, how coarse or fine the needle and thread should be, and so on (1-4).

A counted thread pattern should, as a rule, be worked from the center of the fabric out. Mark the center lines and outer edges with a basting thread. It is also good practice to baste around the edges with light thread to keep the fabric from unraveling.

Materials

Fabric. Embroidery can, of course, be done on all types of fabrics, but some are better suited than others. Keep in mind that the fabric and thread used must be compatible and that both should be washable or dry-cleanable.

For crewel embroidery a tightly woven fabric is best. Counted thread work requires fabric with threads that can be counted easily, and some counted work requires even weave (2-1), which has the same number of vertical and horizontal threads per square inch (or per square centimeter).

The fabric for drawn thread work should be thoroughly dyed. To test for this, pull a thread out from the rough edge of the material.

Fabric to be used for appliqué or similar techniques should be preshrunk so that the embroidery will not pull together when washed.

For counted thread work one possible fabric is linen, an even weave, which is available in white or in colors, fine or coarse, in close or open weave, and in pure linen or blends. Antique embroidery was often worked on homespun linen using flaxen or cotton thread (2-5). Basket-weave fabric (2-2), which is double threaded and easy to count, can be made of wool, cotton, or synthetics. Needlepoint canvas (2-3) is made of cotton or linen and can be found in a variety of grades and in various double- or single-thread patterns. It is stiffly starched and is used for cross-stitch and other embroidery in which the background is to be completely covered. Aida cloth (2-4) can be made of cotton, synthetics, or jute in many variations; it can be used for counted work in which the background is not to be covered or completely filled in and is sturdy and easy to sew on. Many types of striped and checked fabrics are a good choice for counted work and borders, and cotton fabrics with a three-dimensional waffle weave

2-3

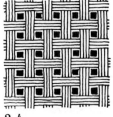

2-4

2-1

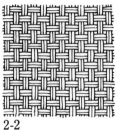

2-2

2-5. *Detail of an old embroidery worked on homespun linen. This example is embroidered with cotton embroidery floss, but homespun flaxen thread was also used.*

are excellent for weaving stitches. Etamine, a light cotton fabric with a mesh, plain or with a pattern woven into it, is also suitable for counted work.

Threads. The threads used should be well suited to the fabric and selected for the particular effect desired (2-6).

Yarn is usually purchased in hanks or skeins. Amager (mouliné) yarn can be found in countless colors; it has six strands and can be divided as needed. Pearl embroidery floss is a glossy, twisted cotton thread that is easy to work with; the most common sizes, numbers 5 and 8, are available in many colors. Embroidery yarn (marking cotton) can be purchased in a variety of weights and colors. Flaxen thread is also available in several thicknesses and many colors; it is particularly well suited for embroidery on linen. Wool yarn, which is usually used for needlepoint, has four strands. It can be divided by strand and is available in a wide range of colors. In addition there are nonglossy, four-strand cotton yarns (weaving yarn) that can be divided; silk thread, both pure silk and artificial (rayon); and synthetic yarns, to name but a few.

Needles. There are long and short, sharp and blunt needles in many thicknesses. A common sewing needle can be used, but a needle specially made for embroidery has a larger eye and is therefore easier to thread with embroidery floss. It is easier to lead the thread through the fabric if the needle is slightly thicker than twice the thickness of the yarn. Needles with sharp points are used for crewel embroidery and similar techniques. Needles with blunt points (so-called needlepoint or canvas needles) are used for counted thread work and needlepoint, since in both cases the needle must pass through the fabric without piercing the threads of the material. A short needle is, as a rule, easiest to sew with. It's a good idea to keep a supply of different types of needles on hand.

2-6. *Examples of different weights of yarn, embroidered on basket-weave fabric. At the top is a delicate border in which the cross-stitches are sewn with two strands and the outlines with a single strand from a six-strand mouliné (Amager) yarn. The cloverleaf border is worked with two strands of a six-strand mouliné yarn, which produces a light effect. The herringbone border is worked in individual wool yarn and number 8 pearl cotton floss. The dark triangles* and sewn-in satin stitch are done with a single strand of a six-strand mouliné yarn. The two white rows of satin stitch are worked in number 5 pearl floss, and the border between them is in pearl floss number 8. For the couching, individual wool yarn, together with a single strand of mouliné yarn, is used. The border at the bottom is sewn with undivided four-strand cotton floss. This produces a solid border in which the wave pattern stands out sharply.

3

Embroidery Hoops. When doing drawn thread work or embroidery on lightweight fabrics, it can be helpful to put the fabric in an embroidery hoop. These are available in different sizes and of varying quality. An embroidery hoop (2-7) consists of two rings, one slightly larger than the other. The outer ring is equipped with a screw mechanism. Lay the fabric smoothly over the small ring, front side up. Press the larger ring down over it and tighten. Hold the embroidery hoop between the thumb and forefinger of the left hand. Press on the fabric lightly with the other three fingers; this will make the sewing easier.

Embroidery Frames. For larger works, use four-sided frames on which the fabric is held taut by pieces of wood (2-8). The fabric should be stretched evenly. Embroidery is done with one hand over the fabric and the other hand under it, with the frame supported against a surface such as a table edge.

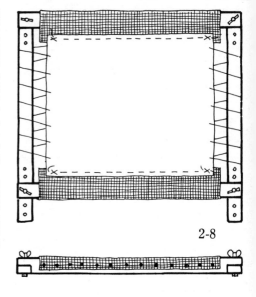

2-8

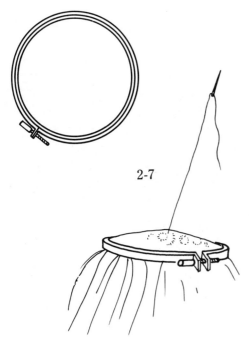

2-7

Make a square embroidery frame yourself with four pieces of wood. On two of them, drill holes on either end and evenly sew or tack on a strip of fabric. On the other two pieces of wood, drill a series of holes on each end.

To baste or tack the piece to be embroidered onto the two strips of fabric, measure from the center out on the wood pieces and the fabric, then baste identical lines out from the center toward the sides. The fabric should be taut and can be attached to the side pieces with strong yarn (2-8). If the embroidery is large it can be rolled up onto the end pieces as it is worked.

Needlepoint Clamp. A needlepoint clamp (2-9) consists of a pincushion mounted onto a screw clamp of wood or metal; this combination is then attached to the edge of a table. It is used when sewing a long seam. Today, this practical device is usually seen only in antique stores, but a similar effect can be achieved by sewing or tying a piece of ribbon or tape onto a firm object. The handwork is then fastened to this strip, which should be long enough for you to work on in a comfortable position.

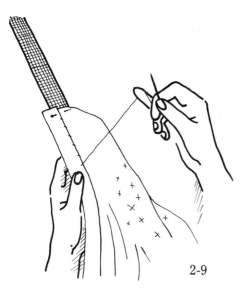

2-9

Scissors. Scissors should be small, pointed, and sharp, especially for techniques that require clipping threads of the fabric.

Thimble. The thimble should fit properly. Blowing into it before putting it in will make it stay on well.

Stiletto. A stiletto is necessary for embroidery in which the threads of fabric are pushed aside in order to form eyelets. At one time, stilettos were made of bone, but today they are usually made of metal or plastic.

The Care of Finished Embroidery

Washing White Embroidery. Soak the piece in soft water and wash by pressing lukewarm soapy water through the material. Rinse several times in clear water. Pieces that are to be functional may need to be washed in hot water, and outdoor line drying is good for the structure of the fabric. When hanging to dry, and ironing, take care not to put too much pressure on the embroidery.

Washing Colored Embroidery. Wash the piece by pressing soapy water through the fabric, being careful not to rub too hard. If you suspect that the colors may run, wash the piece quickly in cold soapy water. Adding a little vinegar to the water will help set the colors. Rinse quickly and immediately roll the embroidery up between two dry pieces of cloth.

Washing Delicate Embroidery. Lay the embroidery on top of a piece of cloth and use a sponge to press soapy water into the embroidery until it is clean. Then place it on a fresh piece of cloth and rinse it in the same manner. Next, place it on a dry piece of cloth and press the water out, using a second dry piece. Allow the embroidery to lie there until dry. If the work is smoothed out well before drying, in many cases it will not need ironing.

Ironing. Before ironing, make sure that the embroidery is lying straight. It should be placed facedown on a soft cloth and can be held in place with stainless steel pins. Iron from the center out, using a thin, well-wrung pressing cloth over the work. Iron until this cloth is completely dry. On wool embroidery, the pressing cloth can be slightly wetter so that the dampness will reach down into the fabric. Quilting, which is usually washable, can be ironed or smoothed by pulling it over the bottom of a warm iron. In some instances it will not be necessary to iron a piece of embroidery at all. Stretch it out evenly and pin it down on an ironing board or other flat surface, placing a damp cloth over it. When the piece is completely dampened, remove the cloth and let the embroidery remain stretched out until it is dry.

Starching. If it is necessary to starch a piece of embroidery, do so while the work is still wet. Then allow the piece to dry and sprinkle it before ironing. Linen should not be starched because this will ruin the sheen and the integral structure of the flax.

Pattern Design

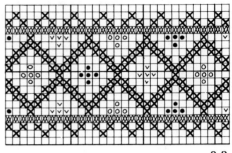

3-3

If you want to design a pattern yourself, or to compile one from some of the designs that you see all around you, it is important to make sure that the pattern you make is compatible with the fabric and yarn in texture and color range. It is helpful to first sew small samples to determine the size and effect of the pattern.

There are several ways to go about designing, whether plotting out a counted stitch pattern on graph paper or transferring a crewel design onto the fabric.

Counted Thread Patterns. Choose a design, or combination of designs, from your own drawings, from books, or from works found in museums.

Outline the shapes of the subject on tracing paper (to enlarge or reduce the pattern, see figures 3-7 and 3-8). Then, using carbon paper, transfer the drawing onto graph paper (you can also transfer the design by blackening the back side of the tracing paper with a pencil). After drawing in the outlines, develop the design—for example, a cross-stitch pattern. In some spots it may be necessary to make changes,

substituting a line of backstitch where a row of cross-stitches would be too thick, for example (3-1).

Either outline each color in pencil and then fill in with colored pencils (3-2), or use a symbol to represent each color and draw this symbol in each block (3-3).

As a rule, this type of embroidery is worked over two threads in each direction, but of course you can also sew over three or more threads. Normally, counted thread patterns are worked from the center out, so it may be a good idea to baste in the center and outer lines (see figure 1-4).

3-1

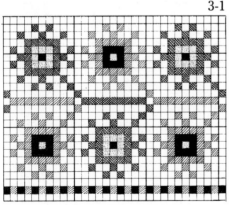

3-2

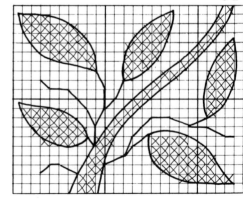

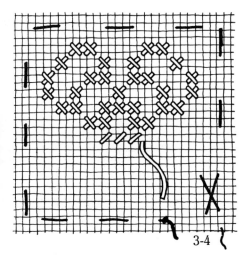

If the fabric on which you want to embroider cross-stitch or other counted thread work doesn't have threads that can be counted, use needlepoint canvas. Baste the piece of canvas over the spot where the embroidery is to be placed, selecting a size and gauge appropriate for the embroidery. Work the embroidery through both the canvas and the fabric (3-4). It may be necessary to pull the thread quite taut—try a sample piece first. After the embroidery is completed, pull the threads of the canvas out, one at a time (3-5). Withdrawing the canvas threads will be easier if you moisten the canvas with a damp, soft cloth or sponge.

3-4

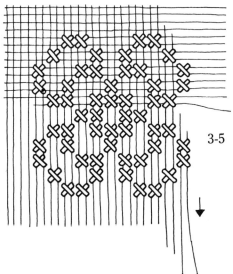

3-5

3-6. *A decorative towel motif from the Danish island of Zealand. The pattern is usually worked in a counted thread stitch, using red or blue thread on white linen. This example was embroidered on smooth fabric with the help of a piece of needlepoint canvas. It is worked in light thread against a contrasting dark background.*

Enlarging and Reducing Crewel Patterns. If you have designed or copied a crewel pattern that is not the size you need, you can make the pattern larger or smaller by using a grid system. Draw a square grid pattern over the design (3-7). Determine the desired height or width of the pattern and mark out this measurement on a new piece of paper, making the same number of square divisions as there are on the original drawing. Sketch the design onto the new grid by placing the lines in the same squares as on the original (3-8).

To make a pattern *taller* or *wider,* draw a grid pattern over the design (3-9). Determine how tall and wide the design should be. Mark out these measurements on a new piece of paper, and make the same number of divisions as on the original, creating rectangles. Transfer the design to the new grid, making it taller (3-10) or wider (3-11).

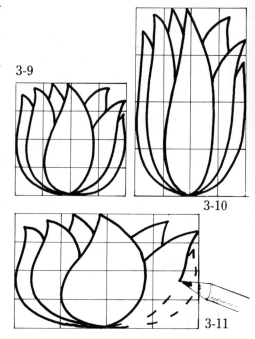

3-9

3-10

3-11

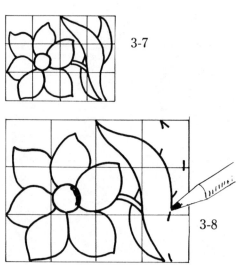

3-7

3-8

Transferring Crewel Patterns. One method is to use *tracing and carbon paper.* A pattern for crewel embroidery can be transferred by drawing it on translucent tracing paper (kitchen parchment can be used). Line the fabric up straight and lay the paper over it, fastening it along the upper edge. You might want to draw guidelines (for example the center lines) that correspond to the threads of the fabric. Place the carbon paper (blue for light fabric, white for dark fabric) between the fabric and the pattern, and trace over the lines of the design with a pencil (3-12). Carbon paper tends to rub off on fabric, so it may be a good idea to remove some of its color with a soft cloth. In some

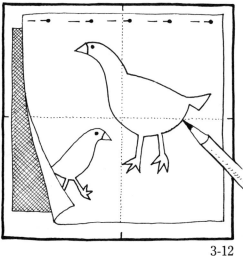

of absorbent paper, with the perforated paper pattern above it. Hold the three layers together on one side with a weight or other heavy object (3-14). For small pieces, use tape.

Using an oil base paint (blue for light fabric and white for dark fabrics) that has been thinned well with paint thinner or turpentine, moisten a rolled up piece of felt or foam rubber. Press the color through the holes of the pattern with the roll. Carefully lift the pattern, and if the

3-12

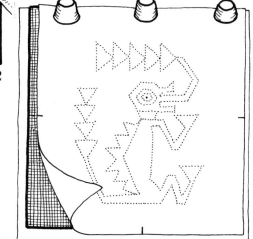

Weight

cases, instead of using carbon paper, it may be possible to blacken the back side of the pattern with a soft pencil.

A superior, but somewhat more complicated transfer method is *pricking out* the lines of the design with a needle (fastened to a stick or in a cork), or with a perforating wheel. A fine needle on a sewing machine can also be used. Draw the motif on a piece of strong, sturdy paper (3-13). Place the fabric on top of a layer

3-14

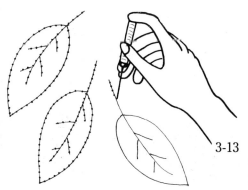

3-13

design is not clear enough, press more color through. Not all fabrics take color equally well, so first test the process on a fabric scrap. The perforated pattern can be rinsed in paint thinner or turpentine and used again. You can use colored powder, talcum, for example, instead of liquid color. Press the powder through the holes, and after lifting the pattern, draw in the design and blow the powder away.

Repeat Designs. For crewel embroidery borders, draw one repeat of a design (or several) and transfer it either in continuous rows (3-15), with mirrored turnings (3-16) or, as an alternative, in a zigzag pattern (3-17). Don't limit repeat patterns to borders—use them in an overall pattern to create a striped effect, for example (3-18).

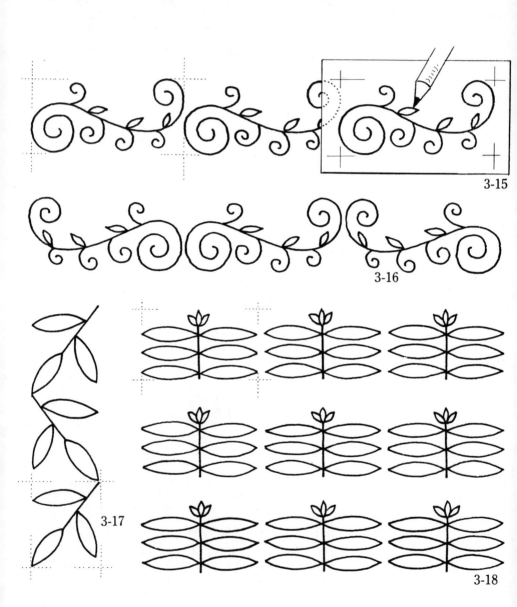

3-15

3-16

3-17

3-18

Curves. Lay out curves by measuring from either a center point or an edge. On an oval or round piece of embroidery, the width of the pattern and its distance from the edge into the center of the piece should be taken into account (3-19). Use a compass or a round object to draw a rounded corner. Transfer the pattern to the fabric or draw it on, constantly checking back to the center of the circle (3-20). Use a pencil, a string, and a nail or tack to mark off borders and designs on a round piece (3-21). Lay out and adjust the pattern in relation to the center point.

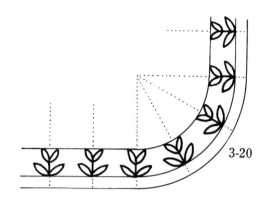

3-20

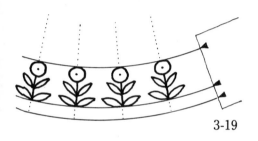

3-19

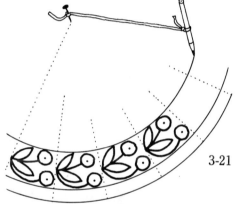

3-21

3-22. *Two border designs. Above: a continuous repetition of diagonal branches worked in stem stitch. Below: a continuous repeat of reversing flower sprigs in chain stitch.*

11

Corners

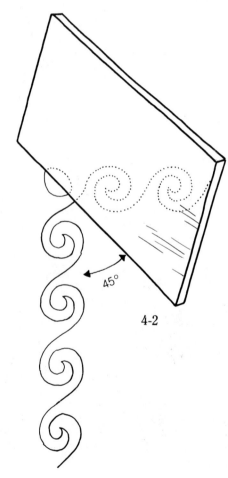

4-1

There are many ways to turn corners in an embroidery piece. You can cut a border and turn it along the diagonal (4-1); it may be useful to hold a mirror up to the border at a 45° angle, experimenting until you find an attractive point at which to make the turn (4-2). Borders can also be continued out to the edge so that they intersect one another (4-3). Or try making the turn at a square section of the pattern (4-4). You can interrupt the border and insert a corner motif (4-5). Or interrupt the main design of the border, inserting a corner design (4-6), and let the edges of the border design intersect one another. With a repeat pattern, rotate the design in the corner a quarter turn (4-7).

45°

4-2

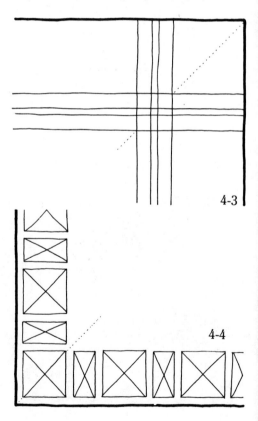

4-3

4-4

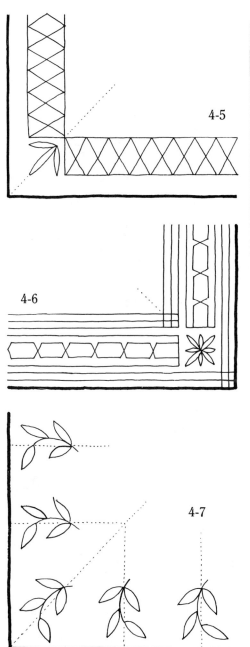

4-5

4-6

4-7

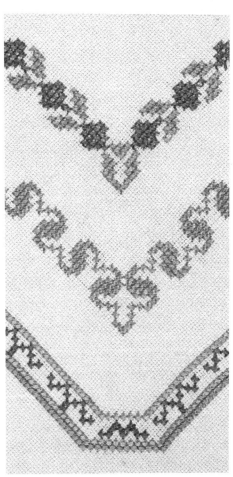

4-8. *Three examples of corners for borders worked in cross-stitch. The uppermost border is a continuous pattern with a specially designed corner motif. The middle example is of a corner turned on the diagonal. The bottom corner is done by interrupting the design and putting in a different motif. The two upper borders are sewn with two strands of a six-strand yarn, so the embroidery has a light look to it. The bottom border is worked in three strands, giving a more solid and distinct look.*

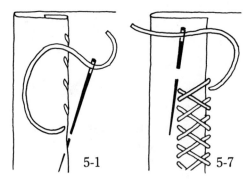

5-1

5-7

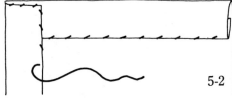

5-2

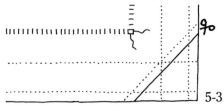

5-3

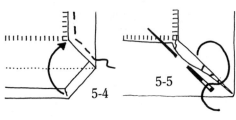

5-4

5-5

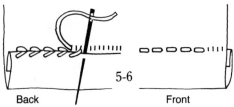

5-6

Back

Front

Seams and Edge Treatments

If you plan to turn a finished piece of embroidery under around the edge, you should use a hemming technique appropriate to the nature of the embroidery and the texture of the fabric. Note that it's often possible to eliminate basting if you press the hem before stitching it.

Common Hemstitch. Turn the fabric under twice. On sheer fabrics, both turns should be the same width. To measure the hem, mark the desired turn on a strip of paper, or use a "hemometer," a ruler specially made for measuring hems. The hemstitches will be almost invisible on the front of the fabric if you take care to take only a little nip of the bottom layer of fabric onto the needle (5-1), but it will be stronger if a larger amount is taken on.

Turning Corners in Hemming. On narrow hems, the corner can be turned straight (5-2). On wide hems, fold the corner fabric under twice and trim away the excess fabric in the corner (5-3). If the hem is being done in a stitch such as antique hemstitch (5-6), pull the threads out all the way to the corner. Turn the hem under (if threads have been pulled out, place the ends in the hem) and baste the hem up even with the threads of the fabric (5-4). Sew the diagonal of the corner together with invisible stitches (5-5).

Herringbone Stitch. On heavy fabrics, turn the hem under once and sew it with a herringbone stitch. Work from the bottom up (5-7).

Rolled Hem. This works well on fine, thin fabrics. Roll the hem gradually while stitching it with an overcasting stitch from the right (5-8). You can also double stitch it (5-9). These hems look equally good on both the front and the back of the piece.

Hedebo Buttonhole Stitch. Working from the left, bring the needle up from the back a little way in from the edge (5-10). Insert it into the loop from the back and pull the thread taut (5-11). These stitches can be worked close together on buttonholes or spaced wider for other applications.

Blanket (Open Buttonhole) Stitch. Turn the edge under and stitch from the left (5-12). These stitches can be used close together to edge fabric that is not turned under—scalloped edges or fabrics such as felt, for example—as well as on hems that have been turned under. They can be worked in various groupings—the combinations are endless.

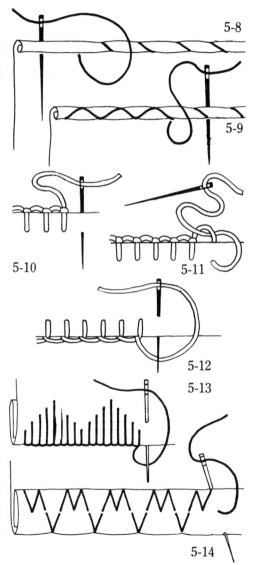

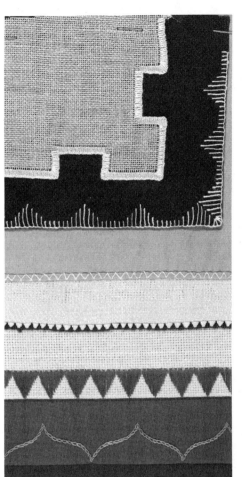

5-8

5-9

5-10

5-11

5-12

5-13

5-14

5-15. *At the top is an edge treatment worked in tightly spaced blanket stitches. Where the embroidery forms a corner, as many stitches as necessary are taken into one hole to form a 45° angle; then the fabric is trimmed up close to the stitches. Below that is an edge done in open blanket stitches worked in groups, followed by a double-rolled hem. Next are two Chinese hems, one with the fabric turned under on the front side of the work and the other on the back side. At the bottom is a hem treatment, drawn on with a template, that would work well on a quilted vest or similar project.*

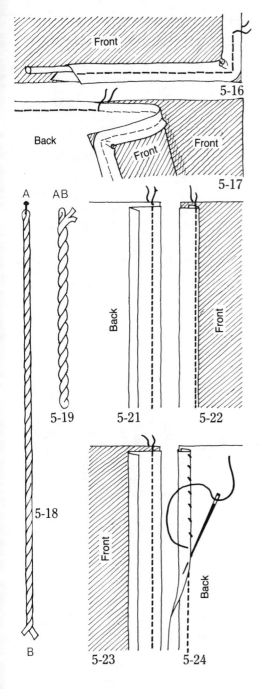

5-16

5-17

A   AB

Back

Front

5-19   5-21   5-22

5-18

5-23   5-24

Chinese Hemstitch. Turn the edge under twice, on either the front or back side of the piece, to the width of the stitching. Use buttonhole or satin stitches (5-13). If the stitches are diagonal, take a tuck into the fabric occasionally in order to keep them in place (5-14).

Piping. This technique, with or without sewn-in cording, can add emphasis and strength to edges and corners. Double a bias tape and stitch it onto the edge of the fabric on the front. The rough edge should face the outer edge (5-16). Insert cording if desired. Then sew the two pieces of fabric being joined together with front sides facing, carefully following the previous line of stitching.

Cording. When cording of a particular color is needed, make it yourself. Take a bunch of threads about a quarter of the desired thickness of the cording and almost six times the finished length, and double them over a pin, tying the ends together with a knot. Twist the threads together—a stick placed between the threads can be used to turn them—until the cord feels taut and firm (5-18). When the cord is taken off the pin, and *A* and *B* held together, the cord will twist up on itself (5-19). Tie the ends together tightly.

Mock Cording. Instead of sewing cording onto the fabric's edge, use a row of tightly placed stem stitches (5-20), possibly worked with several colors of yarn in the same needle. If yarns used in the embroidery are selected, the edging will match the work perfectly.

Bias Seam Binding. If the bias binding is to be machine hemmed on the front of the fabric, place the front side of the binding against the back of the fabric. Machine stitch at the outer edge (5-21). Fold the binding over to the front of the fabric and machine stitch it in place (5-22). If the binding is to be hemmed by hand on the back of the fabric, place the binding on the fabric, front sides facing, and machine stitch them together at the edge (5-23). Fold the binding over to the back and hem it, sewing through

5-20

16

the machine stitches (5-24). When sewing binding onto an edge that curves out, stretch the seam binding slightly (5-25). If the edge curves in, pull in on the binding (5-26). The seam binding can be pressed into shape before stitching. To sew pieces of seam binding together, first unfold them and stitch together, matching up the direction of the threads (5-27). If you find you have to join two pieces of binding while sewing, place the join in the least conspicuous place. Turn the end of the first piece under and sew over it, overlapping the beginning of the new piece slightly with the old (5-28).

Iron-On Interfacing. Heat-bonding interfacing can be purchased in several weights and widths and can be washed or dry-cleaned. Begin by pressing the seam open. Place the interfacing in the seam and fold the hem over. Lay a damp pressing cloth over the fabric, and iron with as high a temperature as is recommended for the fabric. For iron-on interfacing that is backed with paper, open the seam up and place a strip of the interfacing, backing paper facing up, along the edge of the fabric. Iron the strip on with an iron set at medium (5-29). Remove the backing paper, fold up the hem, and iron it in place (5-30). The adhesive can be loosened by pressing with a damp cloth, and removed by pressing with absorbent paper towels.

Overcasting. To join two selvages or folded edges, place the two pieces of fabric on top of each other. Beginning at the right, use overcasting stitches that don't go too far in from the edge of the fabric (5-31). For less conspicuous stitches, work from the back side of the fabric. Work from the front of the fabric for a decorative effect—you might even want to emphasize the stitches by crossing them (5-32) or using double overcasting (5-33).

Dutch Overcasting. This also called the fishbone stitch. Place the pieces of fabric edge to edge, and, starting at the bottom, stitch from side to side using small, close stitches (5-34).

Invisible Overcasting. This is used when the stitches must be as inconspicuous as possible. Sew from the bottom up, stitching from side to side. As much of the thread as possible should be hidden in the folds of the fabric (5-35).

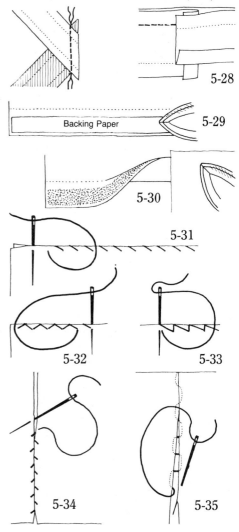

5-28

5-29
Backing Paper

5-30

5-31

5-32

5-33

5-34

5-35

Stretched

5-25

Pulled In

5-26

Decorative Seams

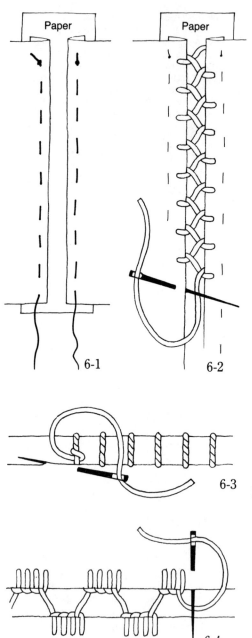

6-1

6-2

To sew fabrics together, lengthen clothing, or inset pieces of fabric, use the bar insertion stitch or other hemming techniques that are appropriate for seaming together two pieces of fabric.

Lengthening. Turn the edges of the original fabric and the piece to be added on under and, if desired, stitch in place by hand or machine. Next, baste both onto a strip of paper, with the distance between them determined by the weight of the fabric—narrow for light fabrics and slightly wider for heavier fabrics (6-1). They can then be sewn together with a variety of stitches.

For a *zigzag insertion,* sew from side to side, working from the outer edge in toward the seam and placing the loose thread under the needle

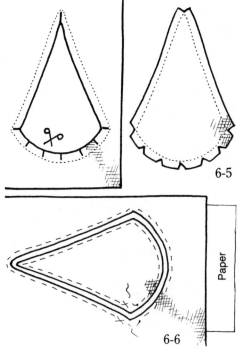

6-3

6-4

6-5

6-6

(6-2). For a *bar insertion*, work one stitch between the edges of the fabric, then go back by twisting the thread one or more times around the stitch, carrying the thread through the fabric to the next stitch (6-3). For a *buttonhole stitch insertion*, sew a zigzag of buttonhole stitches, for example four in each grouping (6-4). You don't have to hem the edges first if you use this technique.

Inset Figures. Cut out a paper pattern of the desired shape. Trace the pattern onto the background fabric as well as onto the piece of fabric from which the inset will be made. Cut out both pieces, allowing for a seam allowance (6-5). Hem the figure first so that it will be possible to correctly determine the size of the hem around the open area. Baste both pieces onto paper (6-6). Use one of the seam treatments described above, or any other technique. A new skirt, for example, can be made by sewing together strips of fabric from two old skirts that were too narrow or too short (6-7).

6-7

6-8. *Zigzag insertion is used here to attach an inset square figure and to do the curved seam. The middle seam is sewn with a bar insertion stitch and the bottom one with a buttonhole stitch.*

These seams become a clever way to enlarge clothing or tablecloths, if care is taken to use the technique appropriate to the color and weight of the fabric. It is possible to sew either straight or curved seams and to inset figures of any shape—either to achieve a decorative effect or to replace a stained spot or a hole.

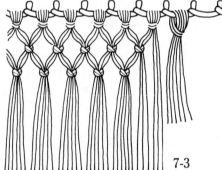

7-1

7-2

Fringes and Pompons

When a woven piece is taken off the loom, it seems natural to braid, twist, or knot together the loose threads at the edges. A similar effect can be achieved by unraveling the edges of fabrics, or by attaching pieces of thread from which a fringe can be made.

Knotted Fringe. Use a needle to make a loose knot, tied from the fabric's threads, close to the edge of the piece (7-1). If you want a thicker fringe, before knotting tie on extra threads between those woven into the fabric (7-2). The unraveled edges of two pieces of fabric can be tied together to make a single fringe, for example at the bottom of a purse.

Fringe with Multiple Rows of Knots. Make a fringe by knotting threads that have been pulled through a border made up of blanket stitches (7-3).

Braided Fringe. This fringe is a four-thread braided one (the two center threads are twisted together first). You can get a zigazg effect (7-4) if after braiding a certain distance you continue by braiding with two threads from one fringe and two from the preceding one. Finish off each fringe with a knot.

Twisted Fringe. Twist two groups of thread in the same direction; two can be done at the

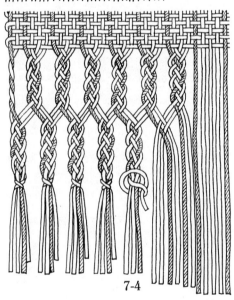

7-3

7-4

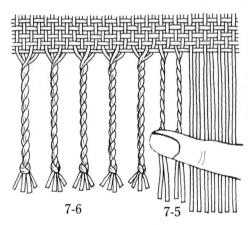

7-6

7-5

same time (7-5). Then twist both together in the opposite direction, finishing off with a knot (7-6).

Tassels. In Greece woolen tassels are tied on the warp end of woven pieces. Wind the appropriate amount of yarn around two fingers (7-7). Cross the raveled threads of the fabric over inside the loop (7-8), and tie them around the tassel before cutting it open (7-9). Trim the bottoms.

Pompons. Use two round pieces of cardboard with a hole in the center. Wind the thread around until the hole is filled in, then cut around the edge (7-10) between the two circles. Tie a strong thread between the two pieces of cardboard before taking the pompons off (7-11). Round the pompon off evenly with a pair of scissors. (7-12).

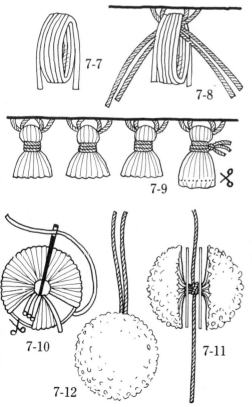

7-7

7-8

7-9

7-10

7-11

7-12

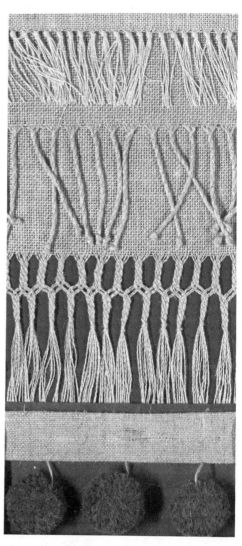

7-13. *All types of fringe can be knotted from either the threads of the fabric or sewn-on yarns. The choice depends on whether the threads of the fabric are suitable, whether the material is large enough, and, ultimately, on what you feel will look the best.*

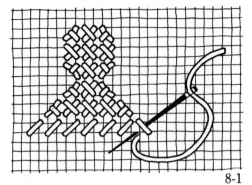

Cross-Stitch

Cross-stitch is a beautiful, refined art form, but if you tire of the rigid step effect it produces, you can make your embroidery even more elegant by using various stitches to create smooth shapes. In the past, no one paid much attention to the direction the cross-stitches faced; today, however, cross-stitches are normally worked so that the top stitch goes from the bottom right-hand corner to the upper left-hand corner.

Half Cross-Stitch. This can be worked over any even number of fabric threads. Sew a bottom row of half cross-stitches and then go back over it with top stitches (8-1).

Three-Quarter and Quarter Cross-Stitches. To work a three-quarter cross-stitch, make the bottom stitch, then tack this down with a quarter stitch (half of a top stitch) (8-2). You can get

8-1

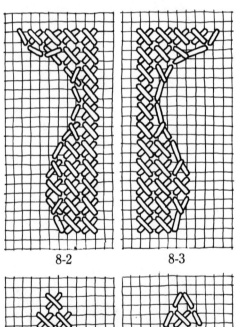

8-2   8-3

8-4   8-5

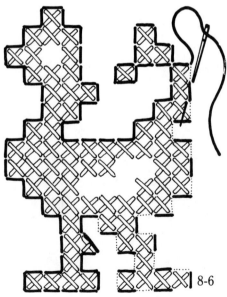

8-6

a different effect if you sew a long diagonal stitch and then tack it down with a quarter stitch (8-3).

Staggered Cross-Stitch. For a diagonal effect, stagger the rows of stitches on top of each other if you wish to form a point. If you want to emphasize the effect produced by the staggered cross-stitches, even off the outer edges by using elongated half cross-stitches (8-4) or by outlining with quarter stitches (8-5).

Outlined Cross-Stitch. For a good effect, sew around a cross-stitch design with backstitches, chain stitches, and so forth, or (probably the best choice) outline it with double rows of running stitches (8-6).

Two-Sided Cross-Stitch. For cross-stitch work that is identical on the front and the back, bring the needle up in the bottom left-hand corner, sew up diagonally, and then go back again (8-7). Next, insert the needle into the center of the stitch and come up again in the lower right-hand corner (8-8). Finally sew a doubled top stitch (8-9).

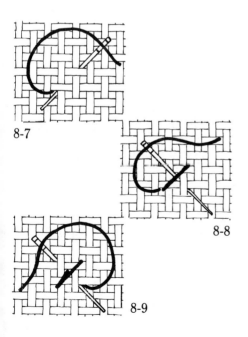

8-7

8-8

8-9

8-10. *In the upper left-hand corner, the figure is worked in staggered cross-stitch, giving it a pointed effect. To its right is a design in which half, elongated, and quarter cross-stitches are used to create contours. The example in the center is worked in regular cross-stitch outlined with darker yarn. This design could have been filled in with half cross-stitches before sewing the outlining stitches. At the bottom is a ball, (left) in which the edges are rounded by half, quarter, and three-quarter cross-stitches; the diamond has even edges worked in half cross-stitches.*

23

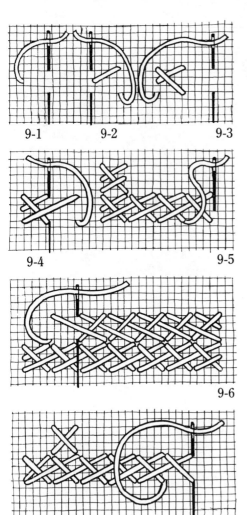

9-1   9-2   9-3

9-4   9-5

9-6

9-7

Alternatives to Cross-Stitch

Many embroidery techniques can be worked using counted cross-stitch patterns as a basis. A few examples follow.

Herringbone or Slavic Cross-Stitch. A good example of this stitch is shown in figure 9-13. It is worked over an even number of threads. Beginning at the left, stitch over four threads, for example, in each direction. Come up in the middle of the left side of the first stitch and take a diagonal stitch to the right (9-1). Sew a diagonal stitch back (9-2). Next, take a diagonal stitch to the right over eight threads (9-3). Sew a diagonal stitch back over four threads (9-4), then a diagonal stitch over eight threads, and so on. Finish the row by inserting the needle in the center of the right side of the last stitch (9-5). Turn the work around and sew the next row in the same manner. But if instead of turning the piece you work the next row from right to left, the effect will be even more braidlike (9-6). Another way to do the herringbone stitch is to begin and end the rows with a cross-stitch (9-7), also working any single stitches as a cross-stitch. This technique is a bit easier and is useful when stitching over an uneven number of threads.

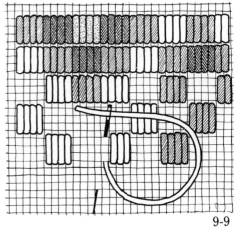

9-8

9-9

Kloster Blocks. This is an old counted stitch that is still popular today; it is usually worked on basket-weave fabric over a certain number of threads in a square, so cross-stitch patterns can be adapted to it. The stitches on the front are parallel with the threads of the fabric. The pattern can be graduated (9-8) and cover the fabric either completely or just partially (9-9).

Plush Effect. This is achieved by working with a yarn that will give either a velvetlike or a coarser, carpetlike nap. Begin at the left and work down over two threads, for example, in each direction. Come up in the bottom left-hand corner and sew a diagonal stitch to the right and back again (9-10). Next, take a vertical stitch to the right with the needle under the thread (9-11). Pull the thread taut, but leave the loop. Finally, take a diagonal stitch to the left and back again (9-12), attaching the loop with this stitch. The loops can be worked over a large knitting needle and then clipped, trimmed, and steamed. An entire piece can be done in this technique, or just certain parts, to depict hair or the fur of a dog, for example.

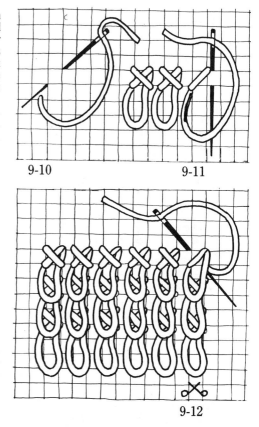

9-10   9-11

9-12

9-13. A herringbone stitch from a piece of Amager blackwork. This piece is worked in black silk on fine, countable linen. The effect of the herringbone stitch is close to that of weaving. This technique is also useful for achieving a patterned effect in vertical and horizontal rows.

25

Pillows

Pillow Forms. These can be expensive down or feather pillows, or inexpensive kapok or foam rubber pillows, (which do, however, sometimes get lumpy). Dacron pillows are light and full and have the advantage of being washable.

Design Placement. Before starting to embroider a pillow covering, determine where the design will be placed. For counted thread work, measure into the center lines and mark them with basting thread. As a rule it is best to do counted thread work from the center out. For crewel embroidery, mark the center of each side on the fabric and the paper pattern. To transfer the pattern, see figures 3-12 through 3-14.

Assembling Pillows. If the pillow's front and back are made of a single piece, fold the fabric at the center, taking care that the distance from the center point to the fold and to the seam are the same (10-1). Since usually only the front of a pillow is embroidered, the back side can be of a completely different fabric. It is important, however, that the front, the embroidery, and the back be compatible for washing or dry cleaning. Whether the pillow is made of one or two parts, whether it is square, round, or oval, it is still sewn together the same way, with the front sides together and an opening for turning, which should be at the bottom. Stitch the sections together with a seam allowance of ½ to 1 inch (1 to 2 cm), depending on how tightly woven the fabric is. On a rya pillow you should incorporate the uppermost row of knots into the seam for the best effect. Turn the pillow cover inside out through the opening. Before turning, it is helpful to fold the seams in each corner over each other; if necessary, they can be held—from the front and the back side—during the turning (10-2). This will result in good, even corners. After inserting the pillow form, which should be slightly larger than the pillow cover, sew the opening shut with invisible stitches (see figure 5-35).

Zipper Closings. You can sew a zipper into the edge of the pillow, but it looks best if it is placed a little way up the back side. Sew it in "invisibly" by machine, or, better yet, with fine

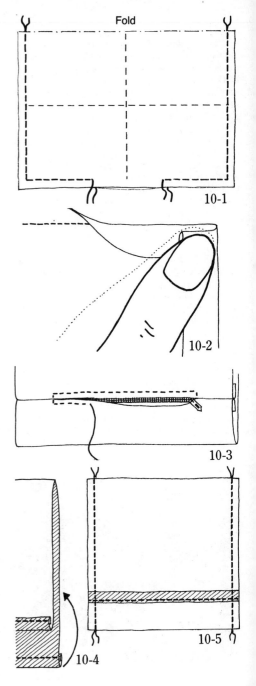

10-1

10-2

10-3

10-4

10-5

running stitches (10-3). When the zipper is in place, sew the side seams.

Overlap Closings. If a pillow is to be washed frequently, an overlap closing is a good choice. An extra 4 to 8 inches (10 to 20 cm) of fabric should be allowed for the closing. Hem both end seams, turning under to the back side, and place the front sides together, with the extra piece hanging below (10-4). Fold the extra fabric up and stitch the side seams (10-5).

Accentuating Edges. Before inserting the pillow form, accentuate the outlines with machine stitching or a row of small running stitches. Further detailing can be done by inserting cording in the edges (10-6). It is easiest to put the cord in at the same time that the seams are sewn. After the pillow form is inserted, complete the decorative stitching and sew up the cording and seam opening.

Strengthening Pillow Edges. Use at the edges. This is made up of a bias strip, sometimes with a thin cord enclosed, which is sewn into the seam (see figures 5-16 and 5-17). Cording can also be used and will hide a slightly irregular seam (10-7); begin stitching on the bottom seam of the pillow. You can purchase the cording or you can make it yourself, particularly if it is difficult to match a particular color (see figures 5-18 and 5-19).

Bolsters. Cut out a rectangular piece of fabric, measured to fit around a rolled-up pillow form; allow enough for the end pieces and possible casing. Sew the piece together lengthwise. If the fabric is lightweight, make a casing on both ends and draw through a strong thread that will hold when pulled tightly together (10-8). If the fabric is heavier, sew a gathering thread into the ends. Pull the thread tightly together and fasten the gathered end. Use a button covered with a bit of the fabric to cover the opening (10-9)

Velcro Strip Closures. Velcro is suitable as a closure on heavy fabrics. The closure consists of two strips of nylon, one with small hooks, the other with small loops. They are sewn on over each other and close with light pressure (10-10). They can be washed in water up to 140° F (60° C) and can also be dry-cleaned.

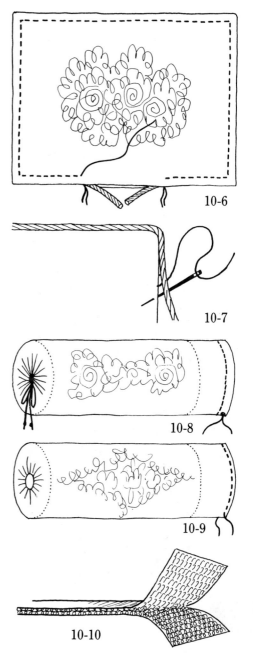

10-6

10-7

10-8

10-9

10-10

Bell Pulls

At one time bell pulls were used to summon household servants through a system of ropes and a bell. Today it is a decorative way of exhibiting one or more rows of a design.

Motif Placement. The motifs should be placed along the center line, allowing for an equal amount of open space on either side. The row of designs should be spaced evenly. As a rule it is best to put the heaviest-looking motif at the bottom.

Fittings. Purchase these before you begin embroidering and mounting the bell pull to assure their compatibility. Fittings are available for small, medium, and large bell pulls, with and without a bell on the end. The top part of the fittings has a little hole or loop for hanging the piece.

Simple Bell Pull. This technique is best suited to heavier materials. Work the embroidery along the center line of the fabric. Sew the piece together with the back side out (11-1), then turn it and sew a casing for the fittings (11-2).

Interfacing. Cut a piece of nonwoven interfacing to the width of the fittings and baste it onto the back side of the embroidery (iron-on interfacing can also be used). Fold the edges under and hem them together at the back of the bell pull (11-3), using invisible stitches (see figure 5-35).

Interfacing and Lining. Baste the interfacing, which should be cut according to the width of the fittings, onto the back of the bell pull. Fold the edges of the fabric under toward the back. Fold under the edges on a slightly narrower piece of lining material and baste, then stitch, the lining in place. Turn under the top and bottom for a casing for the fittings (11-4). Cording may be sewn along the edges. If mock cording is to be embroidered on (figure 5-20), it should be done in line with the threads of the fabric before the bell pull is mounted.

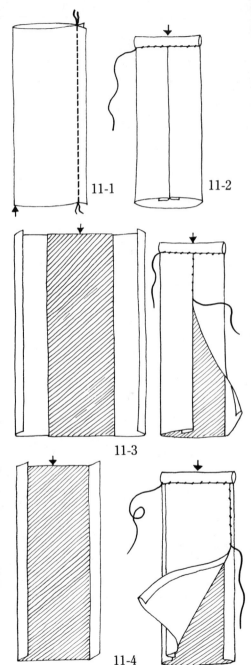

11-1

11-2

11-3

11-4

Wall Hangings

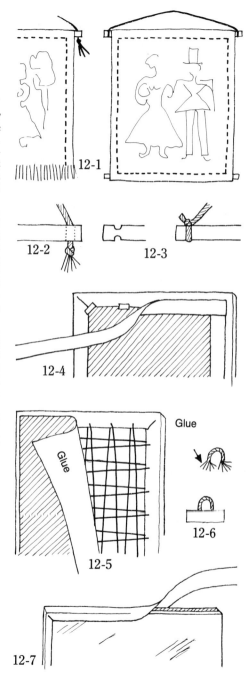

To mount a wall hanging made out of heavy fabric, simply hem around the work, using the top seam as a casing for a dowel or other fitting. The bottom edge can be fringed (see figures 7-1 through 7-5). Wall hangings of lighter fabric may also need a dowel at the bottom (12-1) and can be reinforced and lined (see figures 11-2 and 11-3)

Fittings and Dowels. Fittings can be purchased either singly or in pairs for wider wall hangings, but often a homemade hanger made of a dowel and cord looks better. A dowel, such as a bamboo rod, can be drilled through on both ends. Pull a cord through the holes and hold it fast with a knot (12-2). An alternative method is to cut grooves in the dowel just beyond where the fabric is mounted and tie the cord in the grooves (12-3).

Masonite Mounting. A large piece of embroidery can be mounted on a soft piece of Masonite. Lay the embroidery out evenly on the board. Turn both over and fold the edges of the embroidery under. The edges can be fastened with canvas tape (12-4) or held together with thread sewn from one side to the other and then covered with paper glued onto the back (12-5). Use carpet glue or hobby glue. To hang the piece, fray the ends of a loop of strong thread, glue it down, and tape over it (12-6).

Glass and Cardboard. Cut out a piece of glass and a piece of cardboard, both the same size. Trim the embroidery and place it between the glass and the cardboard. Hold the three pieces together with short sections of canvas tape. Beginning in one corner, pull the tape across to the next corner, fold it around the corner, and continue. The tape can show as much on the front as desired (12-7). To hang, see figure 12-6.

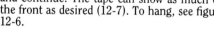

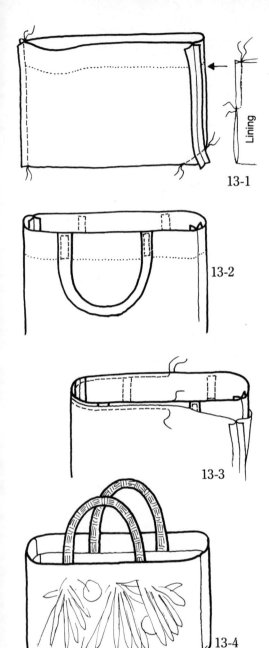

13-1

13-2

13-3

13-4

Handbags

There are many advantages to making your own handbag: you can choose the size, decoration, pockets, handles, and so on that are just right for you.

Motif Placement. Before beginning the embroidery, give some thought to how much of the handbag it will cover. Take into account the bottom, the sides, the catch, the top flap, and so forth, possibly making a paper pattern to work from. Measure out the fabric and baste in center lines to use for the embroidery. Some examples of handbags suitable for embroidery follow.

Simple Handbags. Double the fabric, front sides facing, and sew it together at the sides (13-1). Sewing a seam at the corners will give the bag "body." Cut the lining material out to the same size as the bag and sew the side seams, leaving an opening for turning. Turn the handbag right side out and sew on handles made of canvas webbing or strips of the fabric sewn together, attaching them between the bag's upper fold and the rough edge (13-2). Put the handbag down into the lining. Sew the top seams

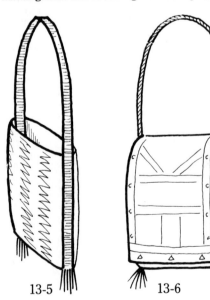

13-5

13-6

with the front sides together, matching seams (13-3). Turn right side out (13-4).

Tote Bags. Sew together a doubled piece of fabric at the side seams. Reinforcements (for example corset stays) can be inserted in the top seam. Follow the instructions given for "Simple Handbags" if you want to add a lining. If you want to use cording, see figures 5-18 through 5-20. A simple tote bag is shown in figure 13-5. A bag with a top flap (13-6) and with a double flap (13-7) can hold an amazing amount. The bag in figure 13-8 is folded over a center dowel, with holes drilled into the ends for the strap.

Handles. Pairs of wooden strips with hidden holes for mounting the fabric and holes for attaching rope handles can be purchased, but these handles are also quite easy to make. Sew the wood strips into the seam between the handbag fabric and the lining, with the side with the countersunk holes facing out toward the front side (13-9). Pull the cords for the handles (see figures 5-18 and 5-19) through and knot them (13-10).

Loop handles should be purchased in a size slightly shorter than the width of the handbag. Turn under the top edge and form casings for the rods of the handle (13-11). If the fabric is too stiff, sew on bias tape to form the casing (13-12). Here the bottom is shown rounded (13-13). If lining is desired, sew it in by hand.

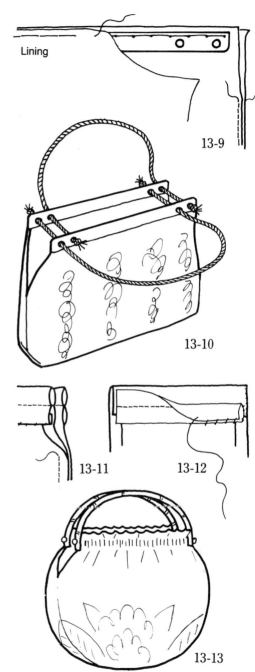

Lining

13-9

13-10

13-11   13-12

13-13

13-7   13-8

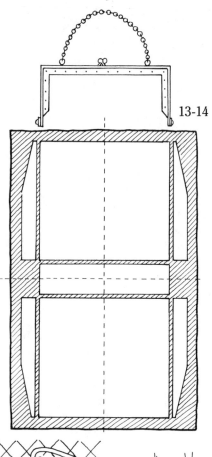

13-14

Metal Clasps. Be very precise when sewing a metal clasp onto a small embroidered evening bag such as the one shown in figure 13-19. On a paper pattern, measure the clasp and the bag's height, breadth, width, center lines, bottom, and sides: if the bottom is, for example, 1 inch (3 cm) across, each side must measure ½ inch (1.5 cm) plus seam allowances. Embroider the fabric, then cut it out according to the pattern, making the lining slightly smaller. On the back side of the outer fabric, iron on pieces of interfacing, cutting out each section individually, possibly with several layers for the bottom (13-14). To emphasize and reinforce the folds where the sides, the bottom, and the front pieces meet, work a row of stem stitches (13-15). Press the outer fabric. Stitch its side seams and those of the lining separately, sewing from the bottom up toward the clasp's hinges. Turn the outer fabric right side out, fold in the corners, and stitch them (13-16). Fold over the edge of the lining and, using small stitches, sew it onto the inside of the clasp, with the needle coming up and going back through the same hole (13-17). Sew on the outer fabric with small stitches, pushing the lining out of the way, and trim away excess fabric at the corners (13-18).

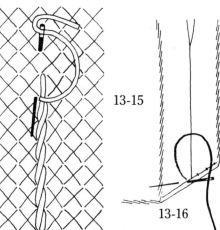

13-15

13-16

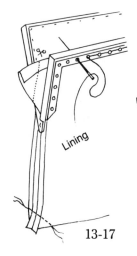

Lining

13-17

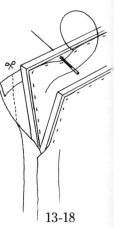

13-18

Rounded Tote Bags. A rope closure is well suited to a baglike tote made of fabric or thin leather. Begin by sewing the bag together at the side seam. Draw a pattern for a round bottom (13-20), remembering to include a seam allowance. If you are using fabric, sew the bottom on by machine. When working with leather, it is best to fasten the bottom on in at least four places with thread or pins and then stitch it in place with small overcasting stitches while holding the bottom in slightly (13-2); the seam can then be dampened and pinched smooth. If the bag is made of fabric, turn the top under and sew a casing at the upper edges. For leather, fold the upper edge over onto the front side and stitch it down by hand, cutting two holes for the handle. First pull one strip of leather or cording (see figures 5-18 and 5-19) through (13-22), then pull the other one through from the opposite side (13-23). If the leather or fabric is too stiff to form a casing, you can sew rings for the cord onto the upper edge (13-24).

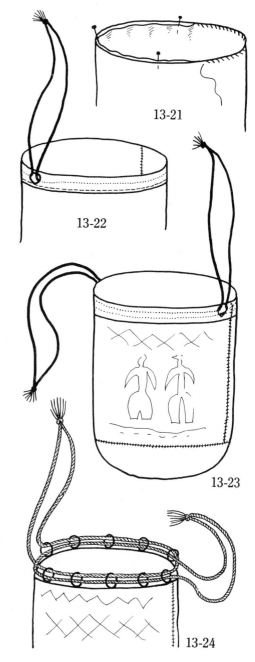

13-21

13-22

13-23

13-24

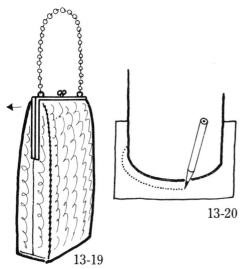

13-20

13-19

ABCDEFGHIJKLMNOPQRSTUVWXYZÆØÅ 1234567889

ABCDEFGHIJKLMNOPQRSTUVWXY-Z
ÆØÅ 1234567890

ABCDEFGHIJKLMNOPQR
STUVWXYZÆØÅ OIOIO

1234567890

ABCDEFGHIJKL
MNOPQRSTUVX
YZÆØ 123456789

abcdefghijklmnopqr
stuvwxyzæøå

Alphabets

Counted Thread Work. The backstitch and the cross-stitch alphabets shown in figure 14-1 can be used to add text to a design or to create monograms or names to be used as part of a border design, for example. It is always a good idea to plot out the text on graph paper first in order to calculate the distance between the letters and words, to measure the distance from the fabric's edge or from other designs, and to see how the work should be laid out in relation to the center lines of the piece in order to create as harmonious an effect as possible.

If more decorative letters are needed, perhaps for a monogram, take the basic form of these letters and elaborate on them in various ways. For example, letters can be made thicker and decorated with scrolls (14-2), the decoration

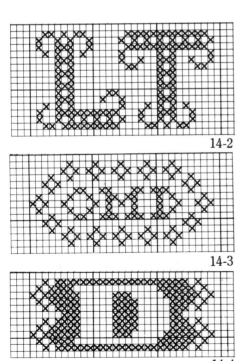

14-2

14-3

14-4

14-5. *Examples of decorative letters. At the top is an intertwined monogram, placed between the date and the year of the embroidery. Below that is a monogram set into a border. Next are broadly outlined backstitch letters filled in with a pattern worked in a finer thread. At the bottom, a name and age are worked into a border design.*

35

can be framed with a border (14-3), or the letters can appear in reverse against a filled-in background (14-4). See the instructions in figures 3-4 and 3-5 to sew counted thread letters on fabric with threads that can't be counted.

Crewel Embroidery. There are endless uses for crewel embroidery alphabets, from clearly marking who owns various items to complicated and decorative designs. A name written out in a simple manner can form a link between the practical and the decorative, especially if it is embellished in some way (14-6).

Figure 14-7 shows an old-fashioned crewel alphabet. This alphabet can also be done in satin stitch (English embroidery, with or without basting underneath) or similar techniques. The letters can be drawn without the double line and sewn in the stem stitch. They can be simplified or made more elaborate with great curlicues. For transferring and enlarging, see figures 3-7 through 3-14.

Monograms. In earlier times, identifying marks, often in the form of monograms, were sewn onto all kinds of articles. Monograms can be put in a row, intertwined, enclosed in a frame, or placed inside a shield shape, for example. Anything goes—but the letters should

14-6

14-8

14-7

36

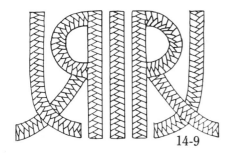

14-9

be legible. An example of intertwined letters is shown at the bottom of figure 14-11. Initials put side by side, sharing common lines, are shown in figure 14-8.

For mirror-image monograms (14-9), the letters are flipped over at the center axis. Not all initials are equally easy to put together, but if one of them is symmetrical, begin by drawing that one. From the center of this letter, draw one or more additonal letters on one side, then fold the paper down the center and repeat the drawing. This example is very simple, but earlier mirror-image monograms were often complicated puzzles. If you want to draw a more complicated mirror monogram, be careful that the angles at the intersections aren't too sharp (14-10). The letters should appear to actually intertwine in the embroidery, with the thicker strokes on top where they intersect. A mirror can be very helpful in working out a pleasing effect.

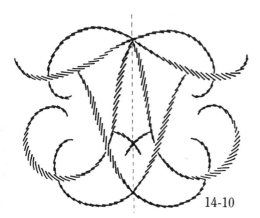

14-10

14-11. *The letter B in the top monogram is sewn in cross-stitch and the decorative curls with stem stitch. The letter E is sewn in stem stitch and the background is filled in with doubled running and herringbone stitches. The intertwined monogram at the bottom is sewn with Portuguese knotted stem stitch, which stays in place well in curved designs; the embroidery is done alternately over and under the lines of the design, giving a braided effect.*

37

Patterns

The important thing is to choose what you like, and there are certainly plenty of patterns to choose from. As an example of the many variations available, even the very simple borders that follow can produce many varied effects.

Closely spaced, vertical stitches have a serious, slightly heavy character, but when sewn in an open form, possibly with warm, strong colors, the effect is lighter (15-1).

In evenly spaced groups, the stitches create an even, regular border (15-2).

A zigzag border looks irregular and festive (15-3).

Horizontal stripes can create a continuous, ribbonlike effect (15-4).

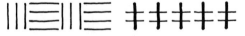

Alternating between horizontal and vertical stitches immediately looks more exciting (15-5).

Diagonal stripes look like they are falling (15-6).

The effect can be changed by placing them in alternating groups (15-7)

or in zigzag lines (15-8).

The variations possible become truly endless if several rows are combined (15-9).

Square stitches give an even effect (15-10),

but it becomes more uneven when they are opened up on one or more sides (15-11).

Triangles can form an open or closed zigzag border (15-12).

Interconnected triangles can produce an amusing running border (15-13).

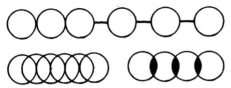

Circles can be varied by spreading them out or letting them intersect with each other (15-14),

or by dividing them into light and shadow (15-15),

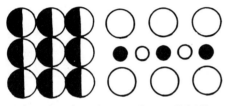

or by using them in several rows (15-16).

Waves are very expressive (15-17).

They can be very even and close, or open and uneven (15-18),

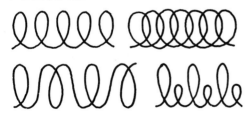

Loops can create a fancy ornamental border (15-19).

15-20. *Examples of variations on a simple form, in this case a wavy line. The top row is sewn with a running stitch, the second and third are worked in couching. The fourth row is a wavy line sewn in stem stitch with French knots, and the next in twisted chain stitch. The very curvy row of waves is done in backstitch. The bottom border is done in the Greek style and is sometimes called a meandering border. This popular border had its origin in the days of Greek antiquity and is named after the Maiandros River, which has a very twisted course. It is done in straight lines and is therefore well suited to cross-stitch.*

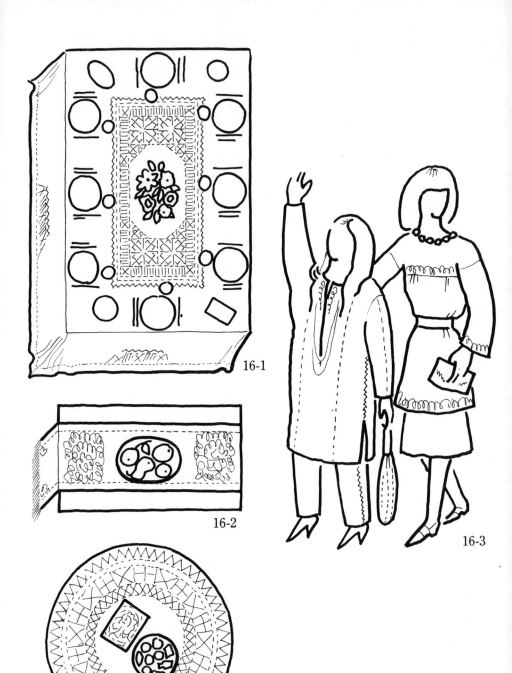

16-1

16-2

16-3

The Placement of Embroidery

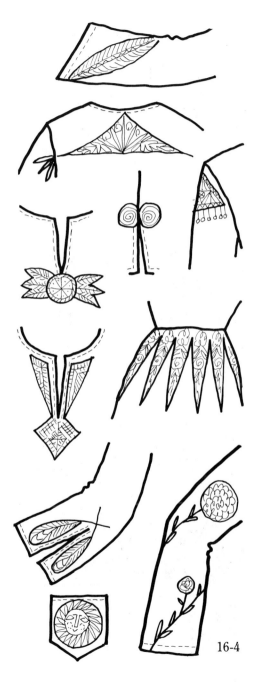

An embroidered tablecloth should coordinate in pattern and color to the dinnerware it will be used with, and it should hang evenly over the four edges of the table. Place the embroidery so that it shows to its best advantage around the plates and other items on the table (16-1). An embroidered runner or table mat should go with the other colors and textures in the room's decor and should either hang nicely over the edges of the table or reach just to the edges— but preferably nothing in between the two. Place the designs in such a way that there is room to rest a lamp, a fruit bowl, or other object naturally on the work (16-2). If working these solutions into the design seems too artificial or commonplace, just throw caution to the wind and do what you think is best—perhaps embroidering an overall pattern on a tablecloth so you can place your plate or cup on a background of roses.

Embroidered articles can have an effect on the decor of the whole room—not only on color and style, but also on shape. To make a low ceiling seem higher, for example, you could make curtains with embroidered or woven vertical stripes or borders. A room with a high ceiling will seem lower if horizontal borders are used; this will also make a small room seem larger, and so on.

This same principle can be applied to embroidery on clothing (16-3). If a tall woman wishes to appear somewhat shorter, she can use horizontal borders or designs on her clothes; and if a short, somewhat heavy woman wants to minimize her size, she can look thinner by using vertical borders and patterns. Designs can be used in an endless variety of ways on clothing, even on old clothes that need to be brought up to date. A lot or a little embroidery can be used, depending on personal taste, temperament, and time available: often a small design on a pocket, along a shoulder seam, on a side seam, or on the sleeves is the most effective (16-4).

16-4

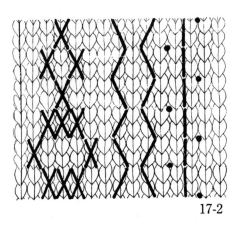

17-1

Embroidery on Knitting

Embroidery on or together with knitting can give a hand- or machine-knit piece a new, smart look.

Counted Thread Work. Sew cross-stitches according to a counted thread pattern using one or, especially on machine-knit works, two knitted stitches to correspond to a square on the pattern (17-1). For an elongated pattern, embroider each stitch over two stitches (in height) of the knitting, or combine it with zigzag stitches, crewel embroidery, French knots, and so forth (17-2).

Stitch Sewing. When adding small designs, monograms, stripes, or similar patterns to a knitted piece, embroider into the stitches of the knitting. Use a blunt needle, preferably with yarn that is slightly thicker and softer than that used for the knitting (17-3).

Freehand Sewing. Naturally, you can embroider a pattern freehand, preferably onto a tightly knit piece, or even onto crochet work. If it is difficult to spread the knitting out to embroider on it, baste a piece of tissue paper onto the back side: work the embroidery into it and then pull the paper away after the work is finished (17-4). You can also use a paper stencil, basting it onto the fabric before embroidering (17-5).

Embroidered Edges. There are many examples of knitted pieces with embroidered edges in old folk embroidery. This is a particularly good idea if you wish to protect a treasured old piece, such as a heavy cardigan (17-6).

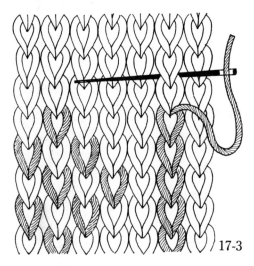

17-2

17-3

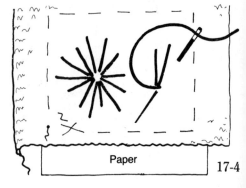

Paper

17-4

Paper

17-5

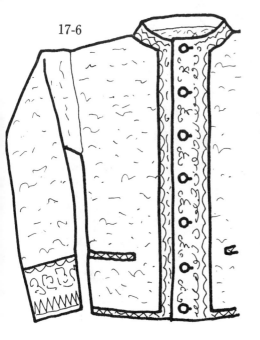

17-6

17-7. At the top is a cross-stitch border done with one stitch of embroidery per stitch of knitting. The stitches all face the same direction. In the center is a small design sewn into the stitches of the knitting. The yarn used is slightly heavier than the knitting yarn. At the bottom is a design done freehand on a background of firmly knitted fabric. In these examples, the knitting and, to some extent, the embroidery were done with homespun yarn—this gives a livelier effect. But if you want a flatter appearance, you can use machine-made yarn.

43

Inspirations from Old Embroidery

If you find a design in a book or a museum and feel it is too complicated or intricate, you can still make use of its individual designs and border patterns.

Figure 18-1, for example, shows one-quarter of the embroidery on the sleeve of a Slovak mourning dress. (The entire motif can be seen by repeating it from the two center arrows.) This drawing reflects all of the irregularities that make old embroidery so full of life. Once you have determined the size of the finished embroidery, divide the area into sections, and draw in and embroider the designs. Use the little leaves, dots, and so forth, as filler.

A repeat pattern (18-2) can be used for a border (see figure 3-15). You can also mirror a pattern on either side of the center line (18-3) or pull out the central heart found in the original pattern and redraw it, preserving its irregularities (18-4). If you don't like the irregularities, draw just one half (18-5) and repeat it at the center (18-6).

18-1

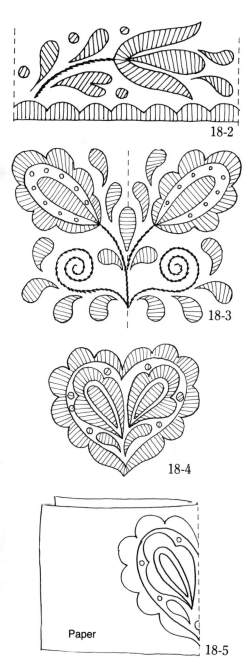

18-2

18-3

18-4

Paper

18-5

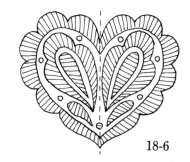

18-6

18-7. *At the top is a detail of embroidery taken from the larger pattern shown in figure 18-1. It is worked in blue on linen in the original satin stitch. The bottom pattern is sewn in an untraditional manner: stem stitches, herring-bone stitches, and French knots worked in light thread on a dark background.*

The Bayeux Tapestry Technique. Tapestries from the sixteenth and seventeenth centuries were usually sewn with silk thread, often in red, on linen, using an outline stitch technique that is easy to imitate. In the Middle Ages, however, the style was more complex. More difficult techniques were then in use, including gold, silver, and bead embroidery on silk. But wool embroidery on linen was also done, and the most famous example of this type of work is the Bayeux Tapestry, which is preserved in the little town of the same name in the Normandy region of France. It is a 70-meters-long and ½-meter-wide picture tapestry depicting the events in England and Normandy around 1066, including the battle of Hastings.

Since the Bayeux Tapestry contains such a wealth of lively and well-composed scenes, and borders filled with stylized animals and imaginary creatures, it is tempting to copy some of its designs—although probably not all 70 meters of it. Many excellent books, with good-quality illustrations, are available on the tapestry. In the Frederiksborg Castle Museum in Denmark, there is even a life-size, full-color photograph of it. The tapestry might inspire you to use the characteristic techniques to embroider events from your own life (for instructions on designing and transferring a pattern, see figures 3-7 through 3-14).

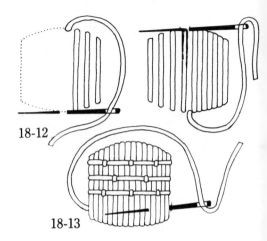

18-12

18-13

The embroidery for the Bayeux Tapestry is on linen, with two-strand wool thread in various shades of red, gold, gold brown, gray blue, dark blue, green blue, and light and dark green. The outlines, sewn first, are usually in a twisted chain stitch. This stitch is worked in the same way as regular chain stitch, but the needle is inserted slightly to the left of the stitch. The stitches are usually sewn quite close together, giving a solid, slightly twisted effect that can be varied in width according to need (18-8). For smaller items, a split stitch is used, resulting in an even, but thinner, line. The split stitch is worked like the stem stitch, but the needle is inserted through the thread at every stitch (18-9). In some places on the tapestry common couching is used. Sometimes it functions as an outlining stitch, with a single outstretched thread fastened down with an occasional perpendicular stitch; sometimes it is worked in a thinner thread (18-10); and sometimes it is used to fill in an entire area (18-11). For flesh color or whenever the linen isn't desired as background, the area inside the outlining stitches is filled in with couching. Thread is stretched from side to side, as it is, for example, in Amager or Delsbo embroidery. The thread is carried across exclusively on the front side, with little nips into the fabric all the way out on the edge (18-12). The most even results are achieved by going across the area twice, filling in the spaces between the first

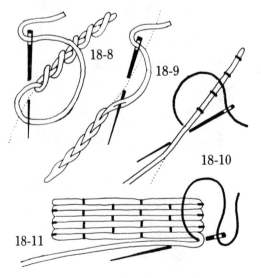

18-8

18-9

18-10

18-11

threads on the second crossing (18-13). The outstretched threads are sewn down with the couching technique, possibly using a lighter thread (18-14). Great variations in the fabriclike effects are made possible by changing the directions of the outstretched threads and by varying the closeness of the stitches used to fasten them down.

With few colors and a particularly simple embroidery technique, a surprisingly lively effect was achieved in this tapestry. For an example of how the figures were distinguished from one another and the variations in the embroidery techniques, see the actual-size drawing shown in figure 18-14.

18-14

18-15. *Use the Bayeux Tapestry technique to create a narrative tapestry of your own. A journey, an event in your life, or your children's adventures, for example, can be depicted in this way. The example here is embroidered on linen with two-strand homespun yarn, like the original work, but if you want a more even effect, you can use machine-made yarn.*

Free-style Embroidery

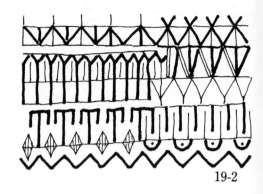

19-2

Even if you want to embroider completely freely, without a pattern or other restraints, you should still proceed methodically. Find materials that are compatible, and embroider them in a way that is appropriate to the final use of the work. Practical items must be embroidered as strongly as the ultimate use of the embroidery dictates. A wall hanging, on the other hand, need not be durable, so for this type of work, cord, tassels, hanging beads, and various unusual objects can be used as decoration, as can decorative seams with long and open stitches.

In the abstract embroidery shown in figure 19-7, advantage has been taken of the various ways that yarns of different thicknesses and qualities twist together when laid in piles against a background. If it is important that the stitches fastening down the twists of yarn be as invisible as possible, use a thin thread, inserting the needle close to where it came up (19-1).

Create a border design by alternating between various stitches and decorative seams done in rows (19-2). This type of design is fun to stitch and has a lively effect when finished.

Start with a simple idea. Embroider a small,

delicate tree (19-3). Then perhaps stitch a strong tree and a weeping willow next to it. Next, the picture seems to need a bush and little hills. You can create an entire woodland scene in this way, adding deer, hunters and dogs, clouds and lakes.

Or sketch some leaves and then sew them directly onto the fabric with one of the outline stitches (19-4). The outlines could be filled in with satin stitch, chain stitch, or other similar techniques. Or the leaves could be sewn onto small patches, which can then be stitched onto the base fabric (19-5). The leaves could also be cut out of various scraps of fabric and appliquéd on (19-6). These last two methods have the advantage of allowing you to move the leaves about until you achieve the placement that looks best.

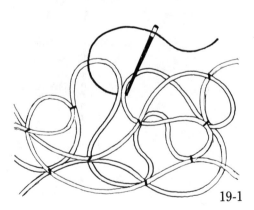

19-1

19-3

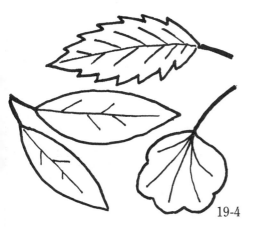

19-4

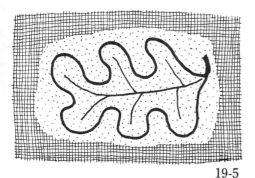

19-5

19-6

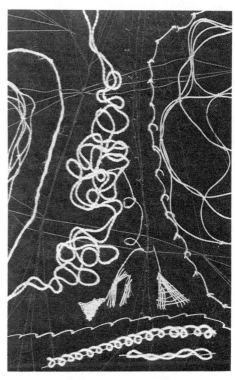

19-7. *This abstract picture has a dark gray background and the embroidery is worked in various weights of yarn in shades of white and off-white. The thin, outstretched threads are olive green. In this example, the composition was begun by laying out various loops of heavy yarn over the background until a pleasing design was achieved. These were then stitched down lightly, taking care not to ruin the twisting of the yarn. A balance was then achieved by adding curving lines of stitching, and using couching, knitted stitches, herringbone stitches, backstitches, and so forth, sewn in very open lines. Thin, green thread was used for long, even stitches in order to emphasize the contrast between the curving and the straight lines.*

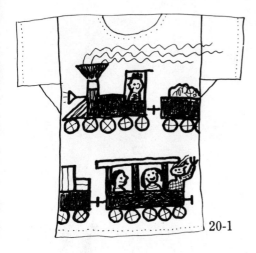

20-1

Embroidery Based on Children's Drawings

Most parents are the proud owners of their children's beautiful drawings. These look good on paper, but when embroidered on fabric, they look even better. Older children can do the design and embroidery themselves.

To begin, draw the design directly onto the fabric or transfer the drawing to paper (see figures 3-7 and 3-8). You can work embroidery on small patches of fabric, which may be easier for a child to work with, and then machine stitch the patches together, as was done in figure 20-5. Using either a whole embroidery or one made up of pieces sewn together, make a wall hanging, adding a dowel and cord (see figures 12-1 through 12-3). Or make the work into a pillow (see figures 10-1 through 10-6). Another idea is to sew the patches together or onto a strip of fabric and make bell pulls (see figures 11-1 through 11-4).

Clothing Decoration. One example is the train on a smock or T-shirt shown in figure 20-1. A pair of jeans can be decorated with grass and flowers at the bottom, with summer clouds on the back and upper legs (20-2). And a light and airy motif with flowers and butterflies is perfect on a summer dress (20-3).

Appliqué. Before embroidering a design with large solid areas of color, consider whether it would be easier to use appliqué for the sky, fields, houses, and such (20-4).

20-2

20-3

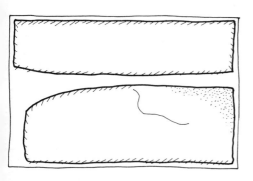

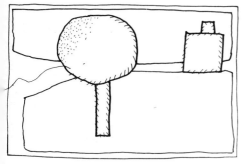

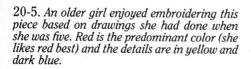

20-4

20-5. *An older girl enjoyed embroidering this piece based on drawings she had done when she was five. Red is the predominant color (she likes red best) and the details are in yellow and dark blue.*

Patchwork

Use large or small patches, depending on how much time you have to devote to the work. The current trend is toward using a sewing machine for patchwork—particularly in making either quilted or lined bed coverings (see page 60).

Mosaic Patchwork—Hexagons. This usually consists of hexagons themselves or the shapes a hexagon can be divided into: squares and triangles. First make a cardboard template of the proper size. To do this, draw a circle on the cardboard and plot out a hexagon by dividing the circle's radius into six parts; then cut out

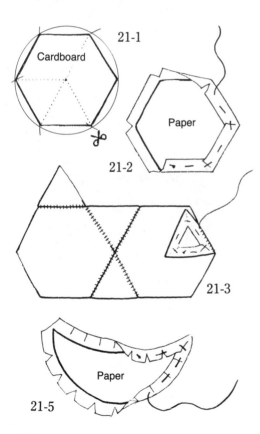

the shape (21-1). This cardboard template can now be used to make paper patterns for the patches. Cut out the patches slightly larger than the paper pattern, and baste around them both (21-1). Join the hexagons, triangles, or squares side to side, using an overcasting stitch (21-3). Be sure that you measure carefully, use a compass and ruler, and baste and sew accurately.

If you sort the patches first according to light and dark colors, it will be easy to lay out a pattern. It can also be helpful to start by cutting out sample shapes from various colors of paper or fabric and experimenting with the design.

Mosaic Patchwork—Free Composition. If you become bored with the somewhat uniform effect of hexagons, you can design your own pattern with more variation, or you might find patterns to base designs on in books or museums. Figure 21-4 shows a detail of a medieval floor tile. It can easily be worked on in smaller sections and later assembled. You could use one or more of the sections, or continue with original designs so that all the sections are different. To sew together curved pieces, clip the seam at the curve (21-5).

An example of a floor tile with a slightly more complex construction is shown in figure 21-6. Starting with a hexagon, draw parallel lines out through its corners, determine the distance to the next hexagon, and draw a circle. The dividing lines of the circle determine the squares and triangles needed. The border in figure 21-7 is based on a Moroccan tile. Square patches are sewn together into strips, which are then assembled. This border could be machine sewn.

Patchwork from Discarded Embroidery. It would be a shame to throw away embroidery

21-8. *Here the hexagons are light and the triangles darker. The combination has an Oriental effect, which is reinforced by the small plant and bird designs worked in satin stitch, stem stitch, and chain stitch. Flowers or small round designs are other possible motifs or the embroidery can be left off—it all depends on the use of the piece.*

21-7

that may be out of style when it could be re-cycled into useful handbags, pillows, or clothes, for examples.

For instructions on sewing the pieces together by hand, see figure 21-3. The pieces can also be machine sewn. To sew squares, for example, determine how big they are to be and allow for seam allowances. Make a cardboard template and use it to cut out the squares. Sew them together in strips and then sew these strips together. There are many variations possible: you could combine large and small squares or stitch the small squares together in pairs before sewing them into the strips (21-16). You can also use triangles, stitching them together into squares. Or sew strips of fabric together, cut them into diagonal strips (21-9), and then sew these together (21-10). The important thing to remember for all these designs is that the cutting and sewing must be done precisely for the result to be satisfactory.

Clothing. To create a stylish piece of clothing, choose old pieces of embroidery that are fairly similar in design and perhaps combine them with solid patches in colors that will give a coordinated effect. For a more exotic look, the more variations in the embroidery and the colors the better.

You don't need a pattern to make a skirt from pieces of cloth sewn together, either horizontally or vertically, and gathered at the waist, (21-11). For more complicated clothing, cut out a pattern—or use an old piece of clothing that has been taken apart—before beginning with the sewing. You will then be able to measure the section and determine how the embroidery can be best be used (21-12).

If you want to make a vest, cut out the outer fabric and lining with adequate seam allowances, sew and turn them, and finish the edges and armholes by hand. Or cut out the outer fabric and the lining without seam allowances and finish off with an edging sewn on by hand or by machine (21-13). When making trousers (21-14) it is a good idea to rip open a discarded pair that fits well to use as a pattern. And how about an easy-to-sew blouse made up of recycled tablecloths (21-15)?

These pieces of clothing should last a long time if you use embroidery and other fabrics that can be washed together. And if they become worn, it is easy to just add new patches.

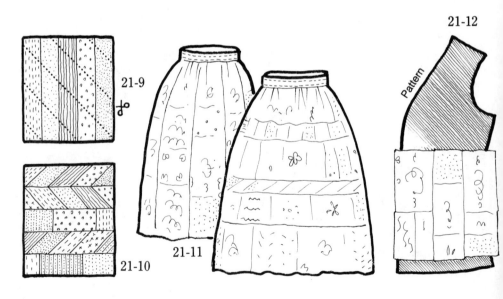

21-12

21-9

21-10

21-11

Pattern

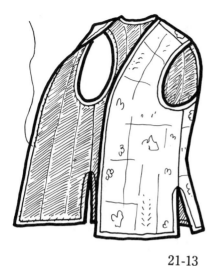

21-13

21-14

21-15

21-16. *Detail of a patchwork quilt made up of large and small squares. A discarded curtain and other old embroidery were used together with small patches of solid-colored fabric. Circles were embroidered on these solid patches. Naturally, any combination of patches, with and without embroidery, can be used.*

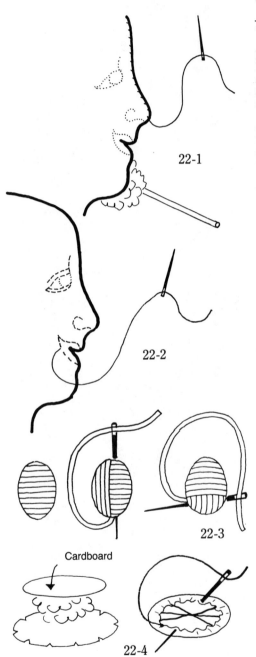

22-1

22-2

Cardboard

22-3

22-4

Embroidery in Relief

For a different look, stuff appliquéd figures lightly with a little cotton, wool batting, or similar material and embroider them with light and dark shading to produce a three-dimensional effect.

The detail shown in figure 22-8 is a good example of how this technique can be used. The figures were cut out, the edges turned under and stitched with the stem stitch, and then the figures were stuffed with a little wool batting (22-1). The facial features and the twigs of the tree are sewn with double running stitches (22-2). The nest is embroidered with random stitches so that the thread resembles the materials of a real nest. Start with a very dark yarn for the deepest part of the nest and build up the edges of the nest with darker and lighter shades. If it doesn't seem to take shape, finish by painting a little highlight on at the ends, using an opaque color. The eggs are made by embroidering several layers of satin stitch on top of each other until a realistic egg shape is achieved (22-3). In order to give the hair some form, it is embroidered in several different shades. The small branches are done in a color that stands out dark against the background.

To appliqué a very small figure, an eye, for example, start by cutting out the shape from cardboard or stiff paper. Place a piece of cloth with a little cotton under the paper and sew the edges of the fabric around the paper (22-4). Begin sewing by forming a cross with a stitch across the back in each direction, then fill in the rest of the stitches. Draw a pupil on the eye and embroider on the eyelashes (22-5).

Bas-Relief. An even more striking three-dimensional effect can be achieved by cutting out two identical pieces of fabric for a figure, possibly embroidering on them, and then sewing them together, front sides facing (22-6). Turn the shape right side out, stuff with as much cotton as needed, and sew the figure onto the background with stitches from the back (22-7).

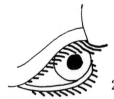

22-5

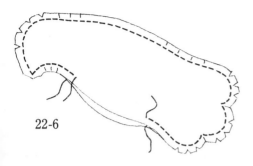

22-6

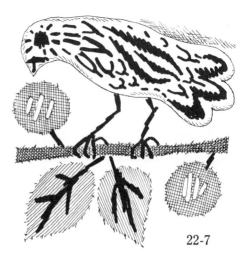

22-7

22-8. For this picture, soft colors were chosen. The background is a matte blue, and various greenish brown shades are used for the nest and tree. The girl's face is yellowish beige, her hair, gray brown. The eggs are light blue.

Pictures from Fabric Scraps

The usual method used to create a picture from scraps of fabric is probably to start with a background and sew on the pieces of cloth, as was done in figure 23-6. It is very important to start out by gathering together enough fabric scraps so that there is a variety to pick and choose from. This is essential for a good finished effect as far as the colors are concerned. Frequently, however, a few colors chosen with care look better than a chaotic mixture of many colors.

Sketch out a full-size design on a piece of paper. Cut along the lines and use these pieces as patterns to cut out the various shapes of fabric that are to be sewn onto the background.

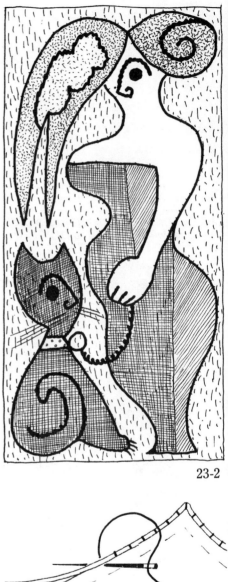

23-2

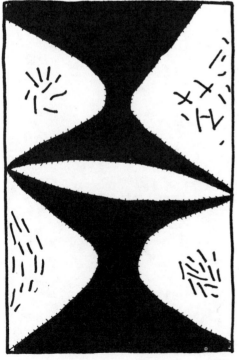

23-1

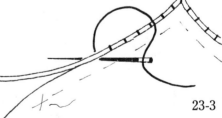

23-3

If the edges have to be turned under during the stitching, be sure to allow extra fabric for this (see figure 21-2). You can also design more spontaneously, cutting out a number of shapes and then experimenting until you find an arrangement that is pleasing—it's just a question of how you prefer to approach things.

Abstract Pieces. Figure 23-1 is an example of an abstract picture that can be done either using the patchwork technique or by appliquéing the pieces on top of each other. To use the patchwork technique (see figures 21-1 through 21-6), begin by drawing the entire picture on a piece of stiff paper or cardboard, then cut it into pieces along the lines of the design. It may be helpful for the later assembly of the pieces to indicate the direction they face, marking arrows on the back of each pattern piece.

Another method is to draw the design on a piece of paper, determine the colors, and decide which pieces will be formed by the background fabric. Then cut along all the lines of the drawing and make fabric shapes to sew onto the background. With either approach, the shapes can be balanced with free embroidery or perhaps additional figures.

Highlighted Outlines. In order to highlight shapes in a picture (23-2), or perhaps emphasize just some of them, you can use a fine or a heavy outline stitch. In this picture, a heavy thread is laid around the figure with hemming stitch (23-3). An even stronger effect can be achieved with buttonhole (23-4) or herringbone stitches (23-5). Eyes, tails, and so forth, can be done in outline stitch or a similar technique.

The picture can be stretched out and mounted on cardboard (see figures 12-4 and 12-5) or finished around the edges (see figures 5-16 through 5-20).

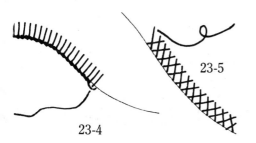

23-4

23-5

23-6. *Even Picasso was inspired by other artists, so why not try embroidering a "Picasso" yourself. Here the tree trunk is greenish brown and the latticework is dark gray. The rest of the work is in shades of green. The vines behind the latticework are slightly darker and cooler in color than those that reach above it. The shapes are sewn on with an overcasting stitch along their turned-under edges. The shadows and vines are embroidered on later.*

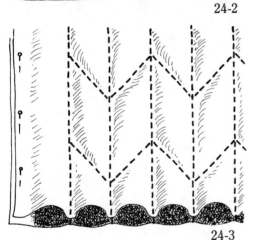

24-1

Quilting

This technique increases the thermal value of a coverlet or a piece of clothing by encasing a thin or thick layer of material between two pieces of fabric. Quilting can be done in several different ways, but the English and Italian are the most common.

English Quilting. This is done with two layers of thin, closely woven fabric around a soft, warm middle layer; in earlier times, this middle layer was usually carded wool, spread out into an even layer, but cotton batting, down, loose pieces of fabric (such as a discarded wool blanket), loose yarn, and various modern materials can also be used. The fabrics, middle layer, and thread used should be compatible—it may help to do a sample piece first.

Larger pieces can be worked in an embroidery frame (see figure 2-8) or in a quilting frame. If the corners of the quilting frame are fastened with wing nuts, a very large quilt can be rolled up along its longer sides. The frame should be placed across trestles or over, for example, two table ends because it is necessary to be able to insert the needle from both the top and the bottom. Put the bottom layer of fabric in the frame, attaching it from the center out to the edge on each side. Spread the middle layer material over it and then baste or pin on the top

24-2

24-3

24-4

layer (24-1). If you don't want to use a frame, sew the quilt together on three sides, turn it right side out, and then put in the center layer as evenly as possible before basting or pinning all three layers together. Sew vertically through all three layers with close running stitches; backstitches can also be used because they produce a distinct, durable stitch, but they are a little slower to work. Sew with strong thread.

Work the pattern out from the center or from a folded edge; it can be made up of parallel lines (which should run diagonally across the direction of the fabric's weave), curves, and all other types of patterns, provided they are evenly distributed without too great a distance between the lines of stitching. A cardboard pattern can be used to trace or baste on the design. The distribution of the middle layer is shown in a cross section (24-2). If the top fabric is sewn loosely to the bottom fabric, the result is a more distinct pattern (24-3).

You can also follow the design in the fabric (24-4). With appliquéd fabric or patchwork, the quilting can follow the various shapes in the work. And last, a soft and warm effect can be produced by tying the two layers together. The placement of these knots must be measured out if there is no pattern to follow (24-5). Sew vertically up and down with one or more threads in the needle; tie the ends together with a knot and clip the threads (24-6). Stitching into a button or scrap of leather will increase the durability of the work.

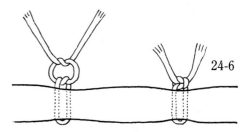

24-6

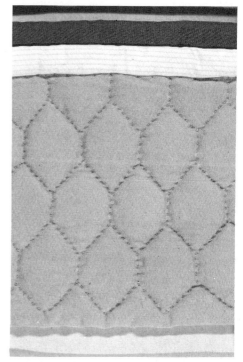

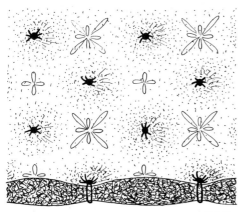

24-5

24-7. English quilting. In this example, the stitching starts at the folded edge. On the other edge a padded edge treatment in other colors has been added. If the quilting is done solidly, it can be washed and ironed—but gently.

Italian Quilting. This doesn't produce as warm a result as English quilting and is usually used for smaller, decorative pieces. Sew the top fabric—for example, silk or a light, closely woven cotton—to a bottom fabric that has a design drawn on it; use small running stitches worked from the back (24-8). Pull thick, soft yarn that is specially made for this purpose between the layers. For the best effect, the design should be made up of parallel lines that allow just enough room for the yarn (24-9). The lines can be placed close together (24-10) or can form a more open pattern (24-11).

Trapunto Quilting. Using the same technique as Italian quilting, follow individual lines of a pattern and then insert cotton or a similar material (24-12).

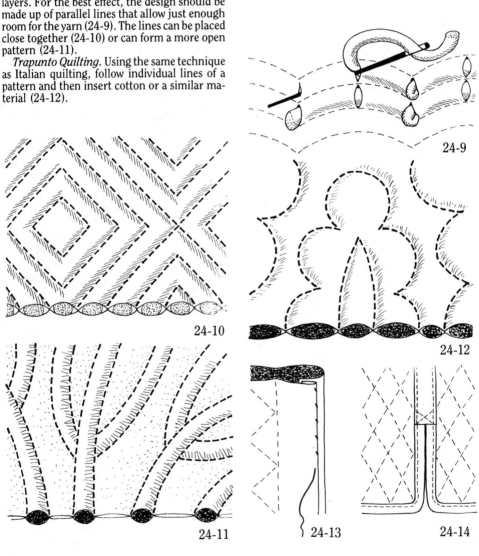

24-8

24-9

24-10

24-12

24-11

24-13

24-14

Edges. If a quilted work is not sewn together and then turned right side out, some finishing must be done on the edges. The top fabric can be turned under over the layer of batting and hemmed onto it (24-13). Or the edges and seams can be finished off with seam binding (24-14).

Edging in Another Color. This type of edge treatment is particularly well suited to pieces with frayed edges or for enlarging a piece. Fold a strip of fabric around some batting and sew it onto one piece of the fabric, front sides together (24-15), then stitch on the second piece of fabric (24-16). Filling can also be pulled through, in the shape of soft cording, after sewing. If the edging is to follow curves and corners, it is best to use a piece cut on the bias.

Doubled Edging. The bottom fabric should be as wide as the full width of the edging; it is turned under to form the outermost edge. Turn this edge under around a piece of batting and baste it onto the bottom fabric. Sew on the next color, fold it over some batting, and so on, until you have the desired width. It can then be finished off as above, or the bottom layer can continue on as part of the quilting (24-17 and 24-7).

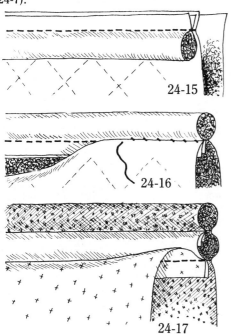

24-18. *Italian quilting. This open-form (24-4) technique can be used for pillows and handbags, for example. The fabric here is pure silk, and there is about ⅕ inch (6 mm) between the parallel rows of running stitches. Follow a design transferred onto the back, and work several stitches before pulling the yarn through.*

Embroidery on Clothing

Quilted Fabrics. A dress or blouse will look more expensive and unusual if it is decorated with a little quilting, for example across the shoulders. Use a scrap from the dress or another fabric, preferably one that is lightweight and compatible in color and texture. Rip open the

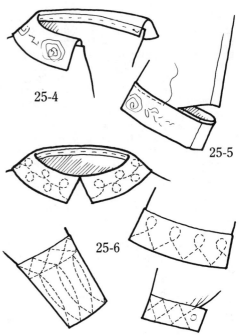

25-4

25-5

25-6

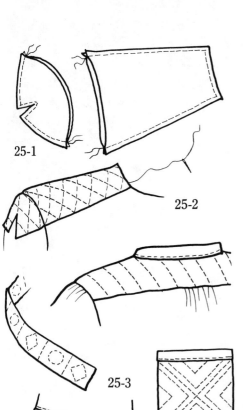

25-1

25-2

25-3

seam at the armhole and cut out a paper pattern for a sleeve cap and shoulder area. Cut out two of each shape and sew them together with front sides facing, leaving the edge that will go into the armhole seam open for turning (25-1). Quilt the sections (see figures 24-1 through 24-4) and sew them into the armhole seam. Attach the shoulder pieces at the neck (25-2). Other uses include quilting on bodices, belts, bottom edges, cuffs, and pockets (25-3).

Separate Collars and Cuffs. At one time it was common practice to use changeable collars and cuff "frills." These protected the edges of shirts and dresses, preventing wear and frequent washings. Today's clothing is not designed to last as long, and it can better withstand washing, but for the sake of variation it is still nice to use separate decorative pieces. They can give quite different effects when used on dark, light, striped, or floral dresses and blouses.

Use a paper pattern based on the measurements of the neck opening and the bottom sleeve edges to cut out the fabric. Stitch and turn the collar and bind the neck opening so that it will be easy to baste the collar in place (25-4). The cuffs can be done in the same way, or, especially if they are wide, they can be sewn together along the side seam and sewn onto the bottom edges of the sleeve (25-5). This is a good way to lengthen sleeves. A decorative pattern can be stitched onto the sections (25-6). It is usually easiest to do the embroidery before assembling the pieces.

Hidden Appliqué. If you are not brave enough to boldly display bright, colorful designs such as jungle birds, roses, or whatever your passion may be, you can sew them onto the interior of a jacket or vest.

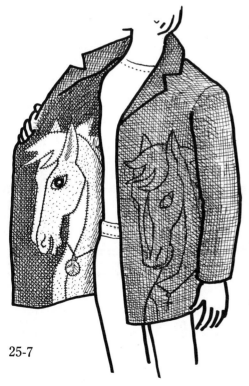

25-7

25-8. How about a cat on your jacket? Or if you don't like cats, a dog, a flower, the sun, or a car—whatever you like. The design shown here is worked by turning under the edges and inserting a little cotton. On a flat figure like this one, sew about halfway around, cut a piece of cotton or similar material out to the correct shape, insert it, and then finish stitching the figure. This cat's features are sewn through both the top and bottom layer of fabric to give them an added dimension. The eyes are painted on, but they could also be sewn on (see figures 22-4 and 22-5).

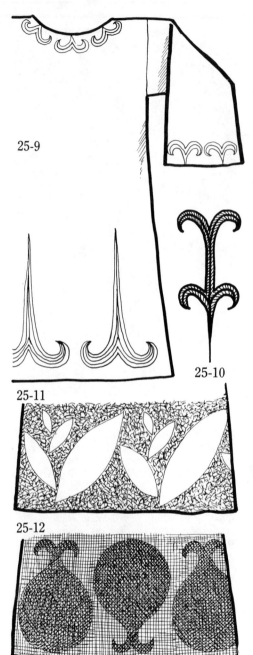

25-9

25-10

25-11

25-12

Cut out paper patterns for the shapes and cut out the fabric pieces, with or without seam allowances; baste them onto the inside of the piece of clothing. If the stitching is done carefully, using strong thread that is of a slightly different color than the garment, or possibly zigzag stitch on a sewing machine, the outlines of the design will appear discreetly on the outside of the piece, as in the jacket shown in figure 25-7.

Embroidery can help make a piece of clothing unique and can emphasize the wearer's personality. Decoration can range from a small design at the neck to an oveall embroidered design; from finely stitched, delicate details and borders to truly bold designs.

Large Motifs. These can alter the appearance of a garment dramatically, whether it is a new piece or one that you have tired of. Sketch a design (see figures 3-7 and 3-8) and transfer it onto the fabric (see figures 3-12 through 3-14). Smaller designs can be designed for the neck and sleeves (25-9) or possibly for pockets, belts, and so forth (29-10). Use stitches that fill large areas, such as the chain stitch or herringbone stitch, or large appliqués, which can be either in bold, contrasting colors (25-11) or in more harmonious shades (25-12).

Sewn-On Embroidery. It is equally easy to appliqué or inset smaller pieces of embroidery onto clothing. All types of embroidery can be used, whether old or new; whether worked with yarn, beads, or cording, or decorated with rivets, fringes, and so on—as long as it looks good together. For example, two identical motifs can be embroidered on opposite sides of an opening. They can be worked on two separate pieces of fabric, which are then trimmed and the designs applqued on. In figure 25-13 they are shown on a bodice, which could either form part of a new dress or blouse or be used as a decorative piece sewn onto an old piece of clothing. A design for the back of a garment could be made up of various smaller pieces of embroidery—experiment with their placement until you are satisfied, then sew them down. You could also cut out attractive designs from old pieces of embroidery (25-14). Long, thin branches of lightweight leather would look nice on a tweed or knit garment (25-15). When sewing the branches onto a form-fitting item such as a sweater, it is a good idea to pin them on while wearing the garment.

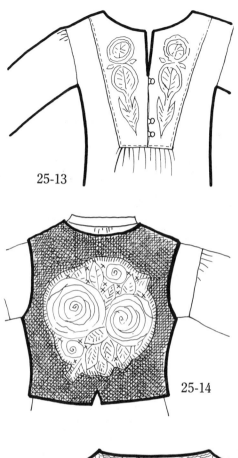

25-13

25-14

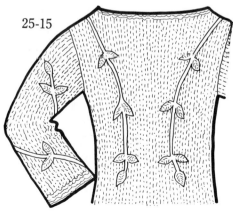

25-15

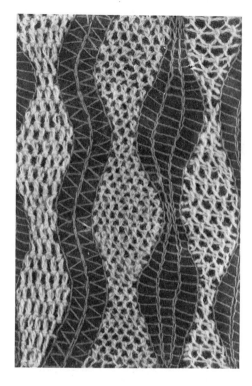

25-16. *A small detail from a long vest that had become a bit faded and drab. It was made new again by embroidering all over it. The light, wavy stripes are worked in coarse, handspun wool yarn in various types of lace filling stitches. The other stitches—chain and herringbone— are worked in lighter-weight wool. All types of clothing can be embroidered, either a lot or a little. Use a variety of colors or a color that matches the fabric, so that the effect is one of structural change. Remove linings before embroidering.*

26-1

26-2

26-3

26-4

26-5

26-6

26-8

26-7

Beadwork

Beads have almost always been known to man, and they have been used almost universally. Museums often have bead-decorated items that can serve as inspirations for your own work.

Materials. Beads and fabric should be compatible in terms of weight and color. Sew the beads on using a long, thin sewing needle. The thread should preferably be the same color as the fabric and should be strong—it strengthens the yarn to wax it occasionally. Place each bead color separately in a flat box so that they can be picked up easily. They can also be placed on a piece of felt or velvet so that they will not bounce out onto the floor.

Open-Weave or Regular Canvas. The beads should cover the fabric completely. Sew in rows, over a two-by-two thread square in the fabric, for example. Take a bead onto the needle and sew a half cross-stitch. The beads will end up at an angle (26-1). The work can be turned around before sewing the next row, in which case all the stitches will lie in the same direction. Cross-stitch patterns can be used.

"Lazy Wife" Stitch. As the name implies, this is an easy technique that can be used on leather, stiff fabric, or felt. Bring the needle up and put six to ten beads onto the thread, insert the needle, and bring it up again (26-2). When covering a wider area, take a small stitch down and up again for every six to ten beads. If you want a three-dimensional effect, roll a pad of material and sew the beads across this.

Bead Appliqué. This can be done freehand or following a pattern drawn onto the material. Use two needles and two threads. Thread the beads onto one thread and sew the row of beads down with the other thread. Sew around the designs first, taking a small tacking stitch across the row every second or third bead (26-3).

Larger Beads. When sewing a row of larger beads, it may be desirable to sew them on more securely. Work with a single thread, sewing back every second (24-4) or fourth (24-5) bead into the preceding bead or two and taking a small stitch into the fabric or leather.

Sequins. Single sequins can be sewn on through their center holes with a bead on the thread (26-6). Sew rows of sequins with backstitches, which emphasize the lines formed (26-7), or with hidden stitches so that they resemble fish scales (26-8).

26-9

Combining Materials. A berry-eating bird done in beadwork is shown in figure 26-9. If you use handmade beads, you may wish to sort them by size, using the smallest ones to make the beak, claws, and legs, the largest to emphasize larger parts, and so on. This bird's eye is made from a sequin and a round bead (26-6). Various types of sequin embroidery (26-7 and 26-8) are used on the wings. And finally, the open areas are filled in with single beads sewn on one by one.

26-10. *Detail of beadwork based on an eighteenth-century bead embroidery. It is worked in a combination of thread embroidery and beadwork, which would be attractive on a contemporary party dress or dressy handbag. The original embroidery was done with black beads and dark thread on a light fabric; here that is reversed. The center stalk is worked in stem stitch and the branches in doubled running stitch or backstitch. The beads are individually sewn onto the threads with an extra stitch (26-4), with the exceptions of the beads on the ends, which are easiest to attach using a small perpendicular stitch (26-3). If you insert the needle as close as possible to where it came up, the perpendicular stitch will be almost invisible.*

Dolls

Jointed Dolls. This is an easy doll to make and since it is assembled from sections, it is bendable. The doll can be made tall, short, fat, or thin, and can be stuffed a lot or a little, depending on whether it is to be cuddly or firm (27-1). Cut out a double piece for each part of the body and stitch together with front sides facing. Hair, lace, and ruffles can be sewn into the seams (27-2). Leave a hole open for turning in every section. Turn using a pencil, or a matchstick for very small pieces. Stuff the sections, sew closed, and sew the parts together with an overcasting stitch (27-3). Beads and embroidery can be used for decoration.

Animals from Rolled-Up Material. These are assembled from cylindrical rolls of fabric, felt, or leather. If it is necessary to reinforce thin legs, necks, and so forth, a pipe cleaner or wire can be placed in the center of the roll. For body parts that are thicker at one end or in the middle, roll the fabric up at an angle (27-4), or roll it around a little cotton or similar material. Trim the rolls and sew them together, preferably with decorative stitches (27-5). To finish,

27-1

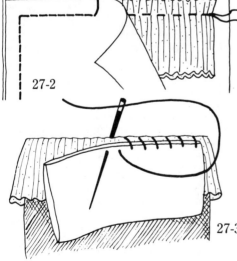

27-2

27-3

27-4   27-5   27-6

stitch the pieces together with overcasting
stitches (27-7).

The giraffe in figure 27-7 has leather ears,
little horns, a short tail, and bead eyes. The
flowers suggest spots. The horse (27-8) has an
appliquéd saddle, wool mane and tail, and leather
pieces as hooves. To make a lion (27-9) roll
lightweight leather. Its mane is made of fringed
leather in a darker color, and it has sharp claws
and a red tongue. The body of the bird (27-10)
is made of two rolls sewn together; the claws
are of wire and the tail of feathers.

27-10

27-9

27-7

27-8

Index

Abstract embroidery, 48–49
Aida cloth, 2
Alphabet, 34–37
Amager embroidery, 46
Animals, from fabric rolls, 70–71
Antique embroidery, 2, 44–47
Appliqué
    bead, 68
    on clothing, 50, 65–66
    fabric for, 2
    and quilting, 61
    stuffing figures, 56–57

Backstitch, *39*
Bar insertions, 19
Bas-relief, 56
Basket-weave fabric, 2, *3*
    and kloster blocks, 25
Basting
    edges, 1
    hems, 14
Bayeaux tapestry technique, 46–47
Beadwork, 68–69
Bell pulls, 28
Bias seam binding, 16–17
Blanket (open buttonhole) stitch, 14
Bolsters, 27
Borders
    cloverleaf, *3*
    corners for, 12–13
    designs, 10–11
    herringbone, *3*
    meandering, *39*
    repeat patterns for, 10–11, 44
Braided fringe, 21
Buttonhole stitch, 14, 59
Buttonhole stitch insertion, 19

Care of finished embroidery, 5
Children's drawings, embroidered, 50–51
Chinese hemstitch, *15*, 16

Closure with overlap, 27
Clothing
    appliqué on, 50, 65–66
    children's drawings embroidered on
        50–51
    collars, separate, 64–65
    cuffs, separate, 64–65
    embroidery on, 64–67
    lengthening, 18
    patchwork, 54–55
    placement of embroidery on, 41
    quilting on, 64
    sewing on embroidery, 66
Collars, separate, 64–65
Cording, 16
    on bell pulls, 28
    on pillows, 27
Corners, 12–13
    hemming, 14
Couching, *3*, *39*, 46
Counted thread pattern
    designing, 6–7
    working from center out, 1
Counted thread work
    alphabets, 35
    fabric for, 2
    on knitting, 43
    needles for, 3
Crewel embroidery
    alphabets, 36
    borders, 10
    fabric for, 2
    needles for, 3
Crewel patterns, 8–9
Cross-stitch, 22–23
    alternatives to, 24–25
    and needlepoint canvas, 2
Cross-stitch patterns, for beadwork, 68
Cuffs, separate, 64–65
Curved seams, 19
Curves, 11

Dolls, 70
Doubled edging, 63
Dowels, 29
Drawn thread work, fabric for, 2

72

Edges
  basting, 1
  embroidered, on knitting, 42
  hemming techniques for, 14–17
  in quilting, 63
  scalloped, 15
Embroidery, placement of, 40–41
Embroidery floss, 3
Embroidery frame, 4, 60
Embroidery hoop, 4
Embroidery in relief, 56–57
Ends, fastening off, 1
English quilting, 60–61
Enlarging crewel patterns, 8
Etamine, 3
Eyelets, 5

Fabric, 2–3
  compatibility with thread, 2
  how to hold while sewing, 1
  insetting pieces of, 18–19
  quilted, 64
Fabric scraps, pictures from, 58–59
Finished embroidery work, care of, 5
Fittings, 29
Folk embroidery, 42
Free-style embroidery, 48–49
Freehand sewing on knitting, 42
Fringes, 20–21

Glass and cardboard mounting, 29

Half cross-stitch, 22
Handbags, 30–33
Hedebo (buttonhole) stitch, 14
Hemming, 14–17
  with Chinese hemstitch, 15, 16
  and basting, 14
  with blanket (open buttonhole) stitch,
    14–15
  corners, 14
  with hedebo buttonhole stitch, 14
  with hemstitch, 14
  with herringbone stitch, 14
  rolled hem, 14
Hemstitch, 14
Herringbone stitch, 14, 24, 25, 45, 59
Hexagons, 52–53

Insetting pieces of fabric, 18–19
Interfacing, iron-on, 17
Ironing finished embroidery, 5
Italian quilting, 62, 63

Jacket, 65–66
Jointed doll, 70

Kloster blocks, 25
Knitting, embroidery on, 42–43
Knotted fringe, 20

"Lazy wife" stitch, 68
Lengthening clothing, 18
Letters, decorative, 34–37

Masonite mounting, 29
Materials, 2–5
Mirror-image monograms, 36–37
Mock cording, 16
Monograms, 36–37
Mosaic patchwork, 52–53
Mounting wall hangings, 29

Needlepoint, 3
Needlepoint canvas, 2, 7
Needlepoint clamp, 4
Needles, 3

Open buttonhole stitch, 14
Outline stitch, 46, 59
Outlined cross-stitch, 23
Overcasting, 17, 52, 53, 59
Overlap closure, 27

Patchwork, 52–55
  clothing, 54–55
  from discarded embroidery, 53–54
  mosaic, free composition, 53
  mosaic, hexagons, 52–53
  picture, 59
  quilt, 55, 61
Patterns, 38–39
  counted thread, 1, 6–7
  designing, 6–11
  mirroring, 44
  repeat, for borders, 10–11, 44

Pearl embroidery floss, 3
Pictures
    abstract, 48, *49*, 59
    from fabric scraps, 58–59
Pillows, 26–27
Piping, 16
Placement of embroidery, 40–41
Plush effect, 25
Pocketbooks, 30–33
Pompons, 21
Practical advice, 1

Quarter cross-stitch, 22–23
Quilted fabrics, 64
Quilting, 60–63
    and edges, 63
    English, 60–61
    Italian, 62, *63*
    Trapunto, 62
Quilting frame, 60
Quilts, patchwork, *55*, 61

Reducing crewel patterns, 8
Relief embroidery, 56–57
Repeat design for borders, 10–11, 44
Rolled hem, 14
Running stitch, *39*

Satin stitch, *3*
Scalloped edges, 15
Scissors, 5
Seam binding, bias, 16–17
Seams
    curved, 19
    decorative, 18–19
Sequins, 69
Sewn-on embroidery, 66
Slavic cross-stitch, 24, 25
Split stitch, 46
Staggered cross-stitch, 23
Starching finished embroidery, 5
Stem stitch, *39, 45*
Stiletto, 5
Stitch sewing on knitting, 42

Stitches
    backstitch, *39*
    bar insertion, 18
    blanket (open buttonhole), 14–15
    buttonhole, 14, 59
    Chinese hemstitch, *15*, 16
    cross-stitch, 22–23
    French knots, *39, 45*
    hedebo (buttonhole), 14
    hemstitch, 14
    herringbone, 14, 24, *25, 45*, 59
    "lazy wife," 68
    outlining, 46, 59
    overcasting, *52*, 53, *59*
    running, *39*
    satin, *3*
    split, 46
    stem, *39, 45*
    twisted chain, *39*, 46

Tablecloth, 41
Tapestry, 46–47
Tassels, 21
Thimble, 1, 5
Thread, 2, 3
Three-quarter cross-stitch, 22–23
Tote bags, 31, 33
Toys, 70–71
Transferring crewel patterns, 8–9
Trapunto quilting, 62
Twisted chain stitch, *39*, 46
Twisted fringe, 21–22
Two-sided cross-stitch, 23

Velcro, 27
Velvet effect, 25

Wall hangings, 29
Washing finished embroidery, 5

Yarn, 3

Zigzag insertions, 18–19
Zipper closure, 26–27